Little Treasures

Gervase Phinn

Dalesman

First published in Great Britain 2007
by Dalesman Publishing
an imprint of
Country Publications Limited
The Water Mill, Broughton Hall,
Skipton, North Yorkshire BD23 3AG
www.dalesman.co.uk

Introductory text, poems and editorial selection
© Gervase Phinn 2007
Stories and illustrations
© the contributors 2007

ISBN 978-1-85568-244-3

Designed by Butler and Tanner Ltd
Colour origination by PPS Grasmere Limited
Printed and bound in China

PUBLISHER'S NOTE
The publisher expresses its gratitude to the children whose
stories and illustrations are reproduced in this book. Copyright is expressly
reserved on their behalf. However, given the nature of the material, it has not
been possible, despite every effort by Gervase Phinn and Country Publications
Ltd, to contact every contributor. In lieu of copyright fees,
Country Publication has made a donation to
the British Dyslexia Association.

CONTENTS

Introduction

In compiling this, the third Dalesman collection, and reading all the amusing anecdotes, insightful observations and wise words of children, I felt reassured that there are so many children out there who are such a delight: entertaining, fascinating, unpredictable, disarming and honest. We read in the papers constantly about difficult and demanding children, disaffected adolescents, teenagers high on drink and drugs, violent youngsters, the poor behaviour of pupils in schools, and we see TV programmes about uncontrollable toddlers and parents struggling to cope with their tantrums and traumas. It is easy therefore to forget that many, many children come from loving, supportive homes, and are in the hands of dedicated and enthusiastic teachers. This collection is a reminder to us all that, on the whole, children are such a source of amusement and wonder.

As with the previous two collections *Little Gems* and *Little Angels* I received so much splendid material that it has been so very hard to make the final selection. Sadly space does not allow me to include all the contributions but I would like to thank all those who submitted their stories and memories, sketches and paintings. It was kind of you to take the time and the trouble to get in touch.

Finally I shall leave you with the words of the late Malcolm Muggeridge, the television pundit and philosopher. They are taken from his autobiography *A Life* and say much better than I why children are such a delight and why we should cherish them:

'Children are the everlasting new start, life springing up again, joyous and undefiled. I know that my children must make the mistakes that I have made, commit the same sins, be tormented by the same passions, as I know that a green shoot pushing up from the earth must ripen and fall back, dead, onto the same earth – yet this does not take away from the wonder and beauty of either the children or the spring.'

Gervase Phinn
www.gervase-phinn.com

Publisher's note

Little Treasures is the final book in this trilogy of children's favourite sayings and, as with the first two books, once again we have been gratified by the submissions from members of the public – especially readers of *Dalesman* and *Down Your Way* magazines – who have shared their favourite family memories and stories. Dalesman Publishing would like to thank everyone who sent in contributions. We would also particularly like to thank all the pupils and teachers of the schools who once again have provided such splendid illustrations.

Mark Whitley, editor

Acknowledgements

The author and publishers would like to thank the pupils and staff of the following schools for their help in providing illustrations: Aston All Saints C of E Primary School, Sheffield; Cayton School, Scarborough; Christ the King RC Primary School, Thornaby, Stockton-on-Tees; Edlington Victoria Primary School, Doncaster; Grassington CE (VC) Primary School, North Yorkshire; Leamington Primary & Nursery School, Sutton-in-Ashfield; Lions Bay School, West Vancouver, Canada; Lydiate Primary School, Liverpool; Town Field Primary School, Doncaster.

The following *Dalesman* and *Down Your Way* readers have very kindly contributed to the text: Anne Austwick; Martin Bannerman; Denise Bannister; Marcia Bannister; Myra Bannister; Margaret Bardsley; Marion Barnes; R Barthram; M Beardshaw; Sheila Best; Richard Billups; Irene Bound; Barbara Bradley; Judi Brown; N Buckle; Jacqueline Buksh; Elsie Burkinshaw; Maria Butterill; Iris Calvert; Don Carson; R & D Carter; J Catherall; Beryl Caunce; Christine Charlesworth; Dorothy Corner; Gladys Crook; P D Davis; Patricia Devlin; Trevor Dorman; Harry Downham-Clarke; Barbara Dowse; Pam Duckett; Marjorie Emsley; George Evans; I Foster; Marlene Gardiner; Margaret Gee; Douglas Gibson; Gerald Gibson; Mike Glover; Jenny Greene; Margaret Griffiths; Joan Ham; Ionne Hammons; Edwin Harrison; Jenni Harrison; J Hetherington; Michael Jenkinson; Muriel Johnson; Joan Jones; Irene Lawrence; Helen Lee; Guy Wolff Litchfield; Isobel and Jack Lovie; Anne Makin; Dorothy Milburn; W Milnes; Rose Mitchell; Elsie Morpeth; Margaret Morrell; Mary Mundy; C Newmarch; John Noble; Shirley Noble; Felicity Oliver; Jean Perry; Christine Phinn; Beth Pickup; Bob Pizey; Moira Rapson; S R Ratcliffe; Christine Reasbeck; M H Robinson; Hugh Rowland; Eileen Saunby; Joan Schmann; D H Shepherd; Heather Simpkins; Annabelle Sinclair; S Slater; Margaret Smith; Alison Staniforth; Joan Stephenson; Faith Steward; A E Swindlehurst; Jane Tarver; Wyn Thompson; Mavis Thompson; Meryl Thompson; David Timmins; J M Tindall; Daphne Toombs; Mary Townroe; Jackie Waller; Miles Walsh ; Delia Waterson; E Watson; Bernard Wilkinson; Douglas Wilkinson; Mavis Wilkinson; A Wilson; A F Willshaw; Daphne Wood

'People of your age are usually in a nursing home by now'

Speaking Their Minds

Children, I have found – and particularly those fortunate to have been born in Yorkshire – speak their minds, as I soon discovered when I visited my very first school in Nidderdale as a school inspector. I sat in the small reading corner to test the children's reading skills, asking one child after another to read to me from one of a selection of books I had brought with me. The choice of *The Tales of Peter Rabbit*, the children's classic by Beatrix Potter, I found to be singularly unfortunate when I asked a healthy looking young man who lived on a farm in the dale to read to me. On that bright sunny morning I came to appreciate just how shrewd, outspoken and bluntly honest children can be.

John, a serious little boy of about seven with large, penetrating blue eyes, was clearly not very enamoured with the title of the book, screwing up his face and shaking his tousled head.

'It's about rabbits, then, is it?' he grunted.

'Yes,' I replied cheerfully. 'Would you like to read a little bit of the book for me?'

'Not really,' he said, observing me blankly. 'But I reckon I've not got much choice. Miss said we've got to read to you.'

'I see.'

'She's been in a reight state this week about yer visit and been in all t' weekend purrin' that display up on t' wall, so you'd better be looking at it.'

'Really?'

'And she's marked all us books up to date and tidied her store room.'

I smiled. 'I see.'

'And she's 'ad 'er 'air done an' all.'

'Shall we start then?' I asked, before he embarked on further disclosures.

The boy read clearly and confidently but with little enthusiasm, and soon arrived at the climax of the story when poor Peter Rabbit, to escape the terrifying Mr McGregor, who was searching for him in the vegetable patch, became entangled in the gooseberry net. The frightened little creature had all but given himself up for lost and was shedding big tears.

'What a terrible thing it would be,' I said, 'if poor Peter Rabbit should be caught.'

'Yer what?' snapped the child bristling. There was a wary, resentful look in the blue eyes.

'If Mr McGregor should catch the poor little rabbit,' I told him. 'Wouldn't it be dreadful?'

'Are you havin' a laugh or summat?' the child's voice hardened. 'Rabbits! Rabbits!' he cried, scratching the tangled mop of hair in irritation. 'They're a bloody nuisance, that's what my dad says. Have you seen what rabbits do to a rape crop?' I answered that I had not. 'Rabbits wi' little cotton-wool tails and pipe-cleaner whiskers and fur as soft as velvet,' he sneered. 'I feel sorry for Mr McGregor spending all that time plantin' and waterin' and tendin' and weedin' 'is vegetables, only to ave' 'em etten by rabbits! I'll tell thee what we do if we see a rabbit on our farm.'

I should never have asked. 'What?' I enquired.

'We shoot the buggers!'

'Oh,' I mouthed feebly. 'Do you really?'

'We don't shoot ours,' interrupted a small girl who had been eavesdropping on the conversation. She had long blonde plaits and the face of an angel.

'Don't you?' I asked.

'No,' she replied sweetly. 'We gas 'em.'

12

Truth Will Tell

A small child was splashing poster paint
On a great grey piece of paper.
'Do you paint a picture every week?'
Asked the school inspector.

The small child shook his little head.
'Hardly ever as a rule,
But miss said we've got to paint today –
There's an important visitor in school!'

When she was four, our granddaughter climbed on my knee
for a cuddle.

'Granddad,' she explained, 'do you know that Ashley's
grandma has died.'

'Oh that is sad,' I said.

'No it's all right,' she told me, 'she's got another one.'

———

I had read in a magazine that rubbing the end of a cucumber on
your face was good for the skin.

'What are you doing?' asked Sue, my three-year-old niece.

'It's supposed to make me beautiful,' I replied, getting to
work with the vegetable. 'Is it working?'

Sue fetched a stool, stood on it and peered at my face. 'Go on,'
she said. 'Keep going, keep going.'

———

I am a classroom assistant and overheard a child of eight addressing the OFSTED inspector who was busily writing, head down, in the corner of the classroom, as the teacher taught the lesson.

'Oi, mister!' he said. 'Miss likes us to listen when she's talking.'

———

My little three-year-old great-granddaughter, Eva, was lying on the floor and systematically kicking her mother's chair with her bare feet. When chastised she just carried on until her mother told her to go and sit on the stairs until she had learned to behave. After a while her mother asked her, 'Are you ready to behave yet?'

Back came the answer, 'No, not quite yet.'

———

The teacher had a large and very realistic crocodile puppet with a zipper for a mouth. When she opened the jaws, inside was a little plastic fish.

'Oh, look, children,' she said dramatically to the infants, 'that naughty crocodile has eaten a fish.' She opened wide the mouth of the creature to show the fish and, turning to a small boy, asked, 'Would you like to take the poor little fish out of the crocodile's mouth?'

'Dream on,' he replied.

———

'Granny seventy?' exclaimed Chloe, 'Gosh, but she's so active. People her age are usually in a nursing home by now.'

———

Walking to town with our grandchildren, we came across a dead hedgehog. We held an inquest and decided it had been hit by a passing car. On returning, to our surprise it had gone. Granddad, in realms of fantasy, said it had gone to the great hedgehog cemetery in the sky.

'Don't be silly, granddad,' said four-year-old James. 'Somebody's probably chucked it in a bin.'

—

The school inspector was examining the book stock in my storeroom one playtime and I, the teacher, went to the staffroom for my morning break, leaving him to it. I arrived back to find Jessica, a six year old, hands on hips, confronting the inspector with the words: 'Only miss is allowed in there, so you can come out.'

—

At the church fête, the young curate came over to have a word with me. We were chatting away about the lovely weather and the excellent turn-out when Maddie, my grandchild of seven, piped up.

'Granny, is this the boring vicar who won't stop talking when he's in church?'

'No,' replied the curate smiling widely, 'it's the other one.'

—

When asked by her mother at the school gates if she had got a harder reading book, the little girl replied sharply: 'No, I haven't if you must know, and it's not as if you always read harder reading books, is it?'

—

'Have you been naughty too, mister?'

There's No Answer to That!

I was reading the story of *The Troll and the Three Billy Goats Gruff* to a group of children in a Bradford infant school. They listened in rapt silence as I told them about the mean and ugly troll, with eyes as big as saucers, ears as sharp as knives and a nose as long as a poker, and how he waited in the darkness under the rickety-rackety bridge for unsuspecting travellers which he would gobble up. All the children, with the exception of a small British Asian girl who sat directly in front of me, listened in rapt attention, their eyes widening at the part where the troll jumped out from under the rickety-rackety bridge. Their facial expressions changed with the story and there was an audible sigh at the end when the Big Billy Goat Gruff butted the troll into the river.

The little girl sat right under my nose, expressionless – not reacting in any way at all but observing me as she might some strange exhibit in a museum showcase.

As I closed the book I asked her, 'Did you like the story?' She nodded. 'Did the troll frighten you a little bit at the beginning?' She nodded. 'And did you feel happy at the end?' She nodded. I found this pretty hard going.

Then I caught sight of the teacher at the back of the room, smiling widely. Her expression said: 'Let the inspector get out of this one.'

It was obvious that this little girl did not find it easy to communicate. She probably had just arrived from India or Pakistan, spoke little or no English and could not understood what I was saying. Perhaps she had special educational needs.

I tried again. 'Did you think the troll would gobble up the goats?' She nodded. 'Can you think of a word to describe the troll?' She nodded. I mouthed the words slowly and deliberately. 'WHAT – WORD – COMES – INTO – YOUR – HEAD – WHEN – YOU – THINK – OF – THE -TROLL?' She stared up at me without blinking. I tried again. 'AT – THE – BEGINNING – WHAT – WORD,' I tapped my forehead, 'WHAT – WORD – COMES – INTO – YOUR – HEAD?' She continued to stare. My voice rose an octave. 'WHAT – WORD – COMES – INTO – YOUR – HEAD – WHEN – YOU – THINK – OF – THE – TROLL – AT – THE – BEGINNING – OF – THE – STORY?'

After a thoughtful pause she said in a clear and confident voice: 'Well, I should say aggressive.'

Question and Answer

'And where do you go on holiday this year, Richard?'
Asked the teacher.
'We went to Mablethorpe, miss,'
The little boy replied.
'And did you go on a donkey?'
Asked the teacher.
'Oh no, Miss,'
The little boy replied,
'On the bus.'

'And what do you do when you get to a full stop?' asked the teacher.

'Get off the bus,' replied the child.

—

My husband had taken our daughter to bed and as a treat was to read her a story. A short time afterwards she came downstairs, settled herself in a chair and said, 'Daddy is asleep now, mummy.'

—

One day the children were looking at the wrinkles on my forehead and enquiring what they were. 'You get them with all the worry children cause,' I answered. 'There is one for you and one for you…'

'And one for daddy!' they shouted.

—

While employed in banking, part of my job was to visit schools and speak to the children. One morning I was keeping an appointment to see the headteacher of a primary school and was waiting outside her office when a very angry and red-faced teacher marched one of her pupils, a small boy of about nine or ten, down the corridor.

'Miss Smith will see you in a minute,' she snapped at the child, 'and she will be very very cross with you when she finds out what you have done.'

On that the little rascal came and stood next to me. Fighting back the tears, he wiped his eyes, sniffed noisily and asked me, 'Have your been naughty too then, mister?'

—

A teacher was explaining that all words beginning with the letters 'ch' always sounded the same, as in 'chin', 'chimpanzee', 'champion' and 'challenge.'

'Not always, miss,' announced a small girl.

'Yes always, Charlotte,' came the reply.

—

A succinct answer to an examination question I once set:

'What do you know about Richard the Lionheart?'

'Nowt.'

—

'There are starving kids in the world, you know,' I told Chloe, aged seven, who clearly was not keen on the contents on the plate before her and stared at the food.

'Yes, I know,' she replied pertly, 'and I'm one of them.'

—

my pet
bee

My niece, Claire, was paddling in the stream fishing for tiddlers when she lost her balance and fell in.

'How did you come to fall in?' I asked her.

'I didn't, Auntie Christine,' she cried, wet through and sobbing, 'I came to catch fish.'

In an English literature examination paper, the candidates were asked to explain the meaning of 'bowels of the earth'. One youngster wrote, 'I don't know about the earth's bowels but I have enough trouble with my own.'

When my grandson was told that he had his shoes on the wrong feet, he replied, sighing, 'Don't be silly, granny, I know that they're my feet. I've always had them.'

My three-year-old son, having been told of the arrival of his baby sister and brought to the hospital to see her, said, 'That's no good at all! I wanted a rabbit.'

'Artificial insemination,' wrote one examination candidate, 'is when the farmer does it to the cow instead of the bull.'

It was my grandson's first day at school. His teacher asked him what his mother called him at home. Was it Nicholas, Nicky or Nick?

'She calls me cheeky monkey,' he replied.

Many years ago a dear friend was teaching at a school in the north of England. The other teachers noticed that a small boy always used a black crayon when drawing pictures. This went on for some time, and my friend was given the task of getting to the bottom of this mystery. Was there some deep significance with his fascination with black? Were there some profound psychological issues here? Finally she delicately questioned him why he only used the black crayon.

He replied bluntly: 'Cos that's t' only colour I've got.'

—

Out driving one day, we passed a large house and country estate. My daughter, aged six, asked who lived there.

'He's a man who races horses,' I told her.

She thought for a moment before replying, 'Oh, then he must be some runner.'

—

I was cleaning my teeth one morning when my five year old banged on the door.

'Is there anyone in there?' she asked. I, with a mouthful of toothpaste, sputtered a garbled answer.

'And is that a "Yes" or a "No"?' came a little voice from outside.

—

When my daughter was about three, I was in a multi-storey car park with her and, as I looked around for the floor number, I said, 'What floor are we on?'

With no hesitation she replied, 'A hard one.'

—

'Grandma, I'll love you till you go to your grave'

The Little Philosophers

I have met some remarkably confident, articulate and clever children in my time who have amazed me with their perceptive questions, astute comments and sharp observations.

In a junior school I met a small girl of about seven or eight, a cheerful, chattery little thing with curly red hair and a wide smile. I soon discovered that she was as bright as a button.

'Mr Phinn, are you very important?' she asked.

'No, not very,' I replied.

'Our teacher told us that you were a very important person.'

'I think she was exaggerating, just a little bit.'

'My grandpa's a very important person,' the child told me.

'Is he?'

'He wears a wig, you know, and a long red dress.'

'Does he?'

'And shiny shoes with high heels and big silver buckles on the front.'

'I see.' I had visions of a drag queen but I suspected I knew what her grandfather did for a living.

'He's a judge,' she informed me.

'Yes, I thought he might be.'

'And he locks naughty people up,' she told me. 'By the way, my first name is India and I'm named after a country.'

I leaned across the table and whispered confidentially: 'Well, my first name is Gervase and I'm named after a yoghurt.'

The child giggled. 'You're not really named after a yoghurt, are you? People aren't named after yoghurts.'

'When my mother was expecting me, India,' I told her, putting on a very serious expression, 'she had a passion for a particular French yoghurt called "Gervais", and for broccoli. I think I did pretty well with the name she picked, don't you?'

'I know what you are, Mr Phinn,' said India, giggling and pointing a little finger at me.

'Do you?'

'You're like my grandpa, Mr Phinn. You're a tease. He's a lot of fun, my grandpa.'

I bet he's not a lot of fun in the courtroom, I thought to myself, in his wig, long red dress and buckled shoes. There would be no teasing then.

'And do you like to be teased, India?'

'Yes, I do rather, it's fun. That's if it's not cruel. Grandpa says you shouldn't tease people about the way they look.

And grandpa says that we're all different and that's why the world is such a wonderful place. "Big or small, short or tall, black or white, dark or light, God loves us all." That's what grandpa says.'

'He's a very wise man, your grandpa, India,' I told her.

India sighed, shook her head and gave me a condescending look. 'Of course he is, Mr Phinn. He's a judge – and a grandpa.'

Dreaming

In the corner of the classroom,
A small child stared at the stuffed hedgehog in the
glass case.
'What are you thinking?' asked the school inspector.
'I was just wondering,' the child replied wistfully,
'What it was doing … before it was stuffed.'

Our young son, David, a charming, impish child, had a habit of telling you what he thought you would like to hear rather than the dull (but truthful) facts. Confronted one day with the stark reality that there seemed to be no escape from being caught out in a lie, he thought long and hard and declared: 'Well, I didn't hear my mouth say that.'

———

'I don't think our teacher knows much,' observed my grandson after a week in school. 'All she does is ask us questions. She's a teacher so she ought to know the answers.'

———

I asked the children to draw a picture of their favourite Bible character. On looking at one drawing, I saw the child had drawn a person wearing a flowing robe covered in circles. I asked who it was. 'It's the Holy Ghost, of course,' replied the child, 'and those circles are the holes.'

———

My grandson Henry was learning his cursive writing. Granddad was trying to help with the homework but Henry would much rather have been out playing football and was making very heavy weather with the writing. Finally he put down his pen with a determined gesture, looked at his granddad and said: 'I hope you live to be a hundred, granddad.'

'That's nice, Henry,' replied granddad, rather moved. 'I hope so too.'

'Yes,' Henry added, 'and then you will get a letter from the Queen and we will be able to see what *her* handwriting is like.'

—

Our grandson, aged five, had just learned to write his name. 'Look, grandma. I've written "James".' He had, but there were two letter As.

I mentioned that one was cockeyed and added, 'And you've put two As instead of one.'

He heaved a great sigh and said scathingly, 'Oh, for goodness sake, grandma.' Then, pointing to the odd one, he told me, 'Can't you see that that one's broke?'

—

Joseph, my grandson, came and sat next to me on the settee, put his arms around me and, giving me a cuddle, said, 'Grandma, I will love you till you go to your grave,' to which I replied, 'That's lovely, and will you put flowers on my grave for me?'

He looked at me and said, 'Yes, of course. And I'll turn them upside down so you can smell them.'

—

An observation by my four-year-old granddaughter, Ruby. 'Granddad, your hair is sticking up like a shark's dorsal fin.'

—

I was complaining one day about all the holes in the back lane on the way to school. My grandson replied, 'But grandma, the holes are supposed to be there. The rain needs somewhere to put its puddles.'

———

After a visit to a farmyard, my four-year-old niece was fascinated by the cows walking up the road.

'Aren't cows clever,' she remarked. 'They can walk and wee at the same time.'

———

Nicola was three when this logical interrogation took place:
Nicola: 'Grandma, were you once a girl?'
Grandma: 'Yes.'
Nicola: 'Grandma, were you once a little girl?'
Grandma: 'Yes.'
Nicola: 'Grandma, were you once a baby?'
Grandma: 'Yes.'
Nicola: 'Grandma, did you have a mummy and daddy?'
Grandma: 'Yes'.
Nicola (quite perturbed): 'Then why did they decide to call you "Grandma?" Grandmas are supposed to be old.'

———

My granddaughter asked me how old I was.

'Oh, very very old,' I told her.

'But how old?' she persisted.

'As old as my hair.'

'Well grandpa can't be very old then. He's got no hair,' she said.

———

On a country walk in the Lake District, Arthur was taken short and had to retreat into some bushes. Gillian, his little daughter, continued walking with us. Shortly after it began to rain and someone joked with Gillian, 'Aw, Gill, why have you made it rain?'

'It wasn't me,' retorted Gillian. 'It's God. He saw my dad having a wee, so He thought He would have one Himself.'

—

When our grandson was aged six, he came on one of his visits and we were sitting on a bench in the garden. As he looked up into the sky he saw a plane go into a large cloud. It seemed to take quite some time before it finally emerged. Before it did he called out to me, 'Granddad, has it got stuck in t' middle or summat?'

—

'Mum, is it the olden days now?' asked Andrew, aged five.

'No why?'

'What a pity,' he said thoughtfully. 'When I grow up and have kids, I can't tell them stories about the olden days.'

—

My son, Dominic, aged six, the little philosopher, often shares his opinions with us. One memorable statement was: 'It's a pity, granddad, that you won't be around for my twenty-first birthday party.'

—

Me: 'What's your knee for?'
Son (aged four): 'A crease in your leg.'

—

38

'He's not my dad – he's my mum's boyfriend'

Oh the Embarrassment!

I think every parent and every teacher has been put in the situation when children have said something which has caused us deep embarrassment.

I had just finished taking the assembly in a junior school in Scarborough, having told the children about the old Viking route known as The Lyke Wake Walk. Legend has it that the Vikings carried the 'lyke' or corpse across the bleak moors to the sea, where the body was given up to the waves.

'Well, I hope you all enjoyed that,' I said cheerfully when I had finished. The children and their teachers nodded. 'Are there any questions?' I looked across a sea of silent children. 'Anything at all?'

'Come along now, children,' came the headteacher's voice from the back of the hall. 'I'm sure there are lots of things you would like to ask Mr Phinn.'

A young frizzy-haired infant with a pale, earnest face raised a hand.

'Ah, there's someone,' I cried, relieved that at least one child had found the story sufficiently interesting to ask a question. 'Yes, and what would you like to ask?'

'What's a condom?'

'Pardon?' I jumped up as if I had been poked with a cattle prod.

'A condom? What's a condom?' repeated the child. I was completely lost for words.

'Well, it's…' I began, looking appealingly towards the teachers.

'It's a snake,' snapped the headteacher quickly.

'No, that's an anaconda, miss,' volunteered a young, helpful, red-headed boy in the senior class.

'It's a bird,' announced a teacher with great assurance.

'Condor,' exclaimed the child at the back. 'You're thinking of a condor, miss.'

The little boy, entirely undeterred, continued with the grilling. 'But what is a condom?'

'It's something you will learn about when you are older,' replied the headteacher firmly.

'Is it a rude word, miss?' asked the innocent.

'No, it's not a rude word, John.'

'Can I call somebody a condom then, miss?'

'No! You certainly cannot!' she snapped.

'Somebody called me a condom, miss,' the infant told the teacher.

'Well, they shouldn't have,' said the headteacher. 'Ignore them.'

'Does it begin with a curly 'C' or a kicking 'K'?' asked a fresh-faced little girl at the front.

'A curly 'C', Sarah, but–' replied the headteacher.

'And is it spelt C-O-N-D-O-M?' she asked, articulating every letter slowly and deliberately.

The frizzy-haired child continued to persevere and still had his hand in the air.

'Right, children,' the headteacher told them loudly. 'Put down your hand now, John. Everyone sit up straight, look this way, arms folded, and when we are ready we can return to our classrooms.'

When the time came for me to leave, I paused at the gate of the small school to marvel at the panoramic view which stretched out before me but was brought out of my reverie by the sound of voices. Out of sight, behind the craggy stone wall which enclosed the school, I observed three or four young boys gathered around the red-haired pupil who had tried to put his teachers right about what a condom was. He was explaining to his fascinated companions that 'You can get them in different sizes, different colours, different flavours…'

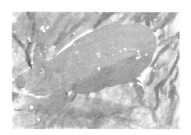

The Inspector Calls

'This work looks most impressive,' the school inspector said,
'So accurate, well-written and so neat.'
'It should be,' said the pupil shaking her little head,
'We've been practising this worksheet for a week.'

There were so many children in Sunday school that the youngest ones had to sit on the wooden floor. A five-year-old boy arrived one Sunday clutching a large family Bible.

'Surely you can't read that, can you?' asked his teacher.

'Nay, I can't read it,' he said. 'I've brought it so I won't get splinters in me bum.'

—

Some years ago I was taking a class and telling the children about Pentecost: 'The disciples were together in a locked and shuttered room when a rushing mighty wind came upon them.'

I asked the children what they would have felt like had they been there. One little lad quickly said: 'I'd have felt like holding my nose 'cos when my granddad lets off wind it smells something terrible.'

—

My four-year-old daughter, in that loud and resonating voice that small children have, announced that she had been 'making cock-porn at school'. Concerned enquiries revealed she had been making 'popcorn'.

—

43

44

My wife and I were spending a quiet weekend at a guesthouse in the Yorkshire Dales when, one evening, a small boy entered the lounge and asked if he could have the television on. He had arrived with a young couple, one of whom was a young man who was sitting in the corner of the lounge reading his newspaper.

'You will have to ask your dad,' I told the child, looking over to the young man in the corner.

'Oh, he's not my dad,' replied the child, 'he's my mother's boyfriend.'

Everyone stifled a laugh as the young man buried his face in the newspaper.

—

I was telling the children in my class about how important water was in our life and how we should do everything to conserve it. I asked them to list the things they could do to conserve this precious commodity. Stop the tap dripping, don't wash the car too often, ban the hosepipe were all suggested. One boy's hand suddenly shot up. 'Miss, you could do what my dad and mum do. They have a bath together.'

—

A child in my class asked me what the word 'dowdy' meant. I was very impressed and asked her where she had come across the word. She told me, 'My mummy says that you wear dowdy clothes.' I was tempted to tell the child's mother on parents' evening what her daughter had said but resisted the temptation and saved the poor woman the embarrassment. I did, however, decide to brighten up my outfits after that.

—

I was in a busy café when a lady came to the next table with her grandson, aged about three or four. When they were leaving, the little boy remained at the table until his grandmother told him to 'hurry up darling and come along'.

The café was unusually quiet when his voice filled the room.

'Here you are, grandma,' he cried, holding up two small handfuls of sachets of sugar and sauces, 'Don't forget to put these in your handbag like you always do.'

—

My two sons, one six and the other eight, watched with interest as a very large woman in front of us negotiated the stairs in the Tube station. Callum, the younger, said in a loud voice, 'Isn't that lady fat, mummy?'

His elder brother, in an even louder voice, told him off. 'You shouldn't say that – it's very rude.' Then he added. 'You should say "obese".'

—

When I was three, the story goes that the local priest called. My mother came to get me, saying, 'Come and see Father Comerford.'

My reply was, 'I'd rather see Father Christmas.'

—

When I was eight years old, my parents were having a party. My sister, brother and I were usually allowed to say hello to everybody before going off to bed. I said in front of a fair crowd of people that it wasn't much of a party without balloons. My father said that we didn't have any, to which I replied: 'Well, there are loads of balloons in the bottom drawer of mummy's dressing table.' I remember being whisked out of the room very quickly.

—

My small daughter asked my friend: 'Why don't you get a bra for your bottom?'

—

At a WI market stall, an elderly gentleman was selling seeds, shrubs and assorted plants. I was with my small grand-daughter, Cecile.

'You plant the seeds,' the man explained to her, 'and then, when they appear, prick out.'

Cecile let out a great 'Aaaaahhhh!' and added 'that's a very very rude word.'

—

I breast-fed both my children. We were in church for the christening of our second child and I was wearing a lovely white silk blouse. When there was a lull in the service my daughter Olivia, aged seven, said in a very loud whisper which echoed around the church, 'Mummy, mummy, you're leaking.'

—

My grandson Anthony was telling me what he had done over the weekend. 'Well, I had a bad cough and went downstairs to get a drink of water in the middle of the night, and – do you know what, granddad? – I found mummy and daddy sunbathing in front of the gas fire.'

—

My grandson, William, and I were on a bus going into Doncaster. A young man got on with a bright T-shirt across the front of which were emblazoned the letters FCUK. William looked at the T-shirt and pondered for a moment before telling me (and the other passengers): 'They've spelt it wrong, granny.'

—

Some years ago we took our fifteen-year-old daughter and four of her friends, all girls, on holiday to Wales. We had hired a cottage for the week, and our daughter and friends, being the age they were, did not want to come with us when we went out so we left them behind at the cottage, which had a nice garden at the rear. With the weather being very nice and sunny, they took advantage of the garden to sunbathe and play their radio. The garden backed onto the garden and house of the man who was the caretaker for our cottage. On the day we were leaving I had to take the key back to him. I knocked on the door of his house and when he answered he had his small four-year-old daughter with him. As I handed him the key, his daughter said, 'My daddy said he will be glad to see the back of you lot.'

—

On a crowded bus the passengers burst into spontaneous laughter when the small girl asked her mother in a very, very loud voice: 'Mummy, what does "bollocks" mean?'

—

My young son, looking at the elegant woman in front of us in the queue, said in a loud voice: 'I think the woman in front must have had plastic surgery.'

—

On the beach little Maisie, aged four, found a condom in a rock pool and, scooping it up in her spade, came to show us.

'Look what I've found, mummy,' she cried. 'Is it a fish?'

Quick as a flash my ten-year-old son Eric informed her, 'No, it's a contraceptive and you should use one for safe sex.'

—

I had taken my class to see HRH Princess Diana when she came to visit our town. Each child was given a small Union Jack to wave and some had brought flowers from home to give to the princess. She smiled at and chatted to the children lining the street receiving their bouquets, which she passed to a lady-in-waiting. She noticed a small boy (he was not in my class but had edged to the front and was standing with us) who was holding a rather pathetic bunch of wilting flowers. I am sure Princess Di warmed to the child, for she came over and took the flowers from him and smiled.

'And have you had the day off school to come and see me?' she asked him sweetly, at the same time ruffling the child's hair.

'No,' he replied, 'I'm off with nits.'

'A murder for my daddy and a lover for my mummy'

Out of the Mouths . . .

'This morning we have a very special visitor in school,' the teacher told her class of seven year olds and gesturing in my direction. I was undertaking a short inspection in a small village school in the heart of the Yorkshire Dales one cold November day. 'And his name is Mr Phinn,' she continued. 'Mr Phinn is just in time to join us for "News time". The teacher turned in my direction. 'Every Monday morning, Mr Phinn,' she explained, 'I ask certain of the children to come out to the front of the classroom to tell us what interesting things they have been doing over the weekend. Do take a seat, Mr Phinn, and then we can begin.'

The first child to speak was a large girl with a pale moon face, large owl eyes and two big bunches of thick straw-coloured hair tied with crimson ribbons.

'An 'edgehog come out from t' bushes last night,' she announced volubly. 'And then it went back in.'

'That is unusual,' remarked the teacher. 'Isn't that unusual, Mr Phinn?'

'Yes, indeed,' I agreed. 'Very unusual.'

'Hedgehogs usually sleep all winter,' said the teacher. 'Did you disturb it, Melody?'

'No, miss,' replied the child. 'It just come out and went back in. We put some bread and milk out for it.'

'Well so long as you didn't poke it and wake it up. Let's have Duane out to the front.' The next young newsgiver was a bespectacled little boy with black hair slicked back and with a neat parting down one side. 'Now, Duane, did anything interesting happen to you at the weekend?'

'Some white worms come out of my bottom, miss,' the boy informed her.

The teacher squeezed her eyes together like someone wincing at an inward pain. 'I really don't think we want to hear about the white worms thank you very much, Duane.'

The child continued regardless. 'My mum went to the chemist to get this pink medicine which tasted like strawberry milkshake to stop these white worms coming out of my bottom.'

The teacher held up a hand as if stopping traffic. 'I think we have heard quite enough about the white worms,' she interrupted. 'Haven't we, Mr Phinn?'

'Yes, indeed,' I replied, attempting not to smile.

'I shall write the word "hibernation" on the blackboard,' announced the teacher, a red nervous rash creeping up her neck, 'and we shall talk about the hedgehog that Melody found in her garden. I am not at all certain, however, that it is a very good idea to give hedgehogs bread and milk, is it Mr Phinn?'

'No,' I agreed. 'It makes their stomachs swell and it is bad for them.'

'Actually,' said the teacher, 'I am not sure what hedgehogs eat. Do you know, Mr Phinn?'

'Yes,' I replied, and then added without a trace of a smile, 'It's worms.'

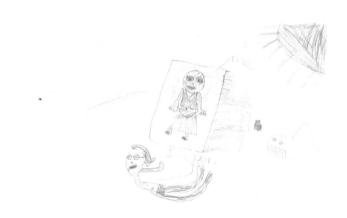

Home

In the Home Corner,
In an infant school classroom,
A boy and girl,
Rising five,
Were arguing,
Stabbing the air with small fingers,
Jutting out their chins,
And stamping little feet.
'Oh, do shut up!'
'No, you shut up!'
'I'm sick of you!'
'I'm sick of you!'
'Oh, just be quiet!'
'No, you be quiet!'
'Oh, do shut up!'
'No, you shut up!'
'What is all this?' the teacher cried.
'Were playing mums and dads,'
The infants both replied.

My granddaughter was fascinated with the dolls in a toyshop.
There were pretty authentic boy and girl dolls. 'Look, granny, at
this one,' she said, picking up the boy doll and scrutinising the
lower regions. 'That's a funny place to have a finger.'

—

My father, whose name was Harry Wood, ran a toy and cycle shop. Every 11-Plus exam time, children were promised a present if they passed to go to grammar school. One young boy had been promised a bicycle, his dream. Luckily he passed and that night on receiving his coveted award he said his prayers aloud as he always did, but his excitement took over and he said, 'Our Father who art in Heaven, Harry Wood be thy name.'

—

On Armistice Day my daughter was in a shop with her son, aged six, when a gun was fired for the start of the two-minute silence. The little lad was intrigued why everyone around him stood still, heads bent. He asked his mother what was happening and she explained that they were saying a silent prayer for all the people who had been killed in the world wars. When the gun was fired again at the end of the silence, he asked: 'Have they shot another one?'

—

Three-year-old daughter, sat in child seat in the back of the car, with mother (me) driving:

Louise: 'Mummee...'

Mummy: 'Yes, dear?'

Louise: 'Why do all the men that you know have the same name?'

Puzzled expression from mummy. 'What do you mean, dear?'

Louise: 'They are all called Dick.'

Oh dear. I have since become a much less aggressive driver.

—

I used to work in a library and every Saturday morning a little boy came in, asking for 'A murder for my daddy and a lover for my mummy'.

———

My five year olds were acting out a famous children's story. A dour little boy was the wolf in bed, disguised as grand-mamma, awaiting the visit of Little Red Riding Hood. His interpretation of the knock at the door and the instruction to 'Lift the latch, my dear, and come in' was typically Yorkshire: 'Cum in an' shut t' dooer – there's a reight draft in 'ere.'

———

My four-year-old granddaughter and I had been enjoying several games of Snakes and Ladders. She followed me into my bedroom and heard me mutter to myself, 'Drat! I've got a ladder in my tights.' At this point she dashed into the kitchen calling, 'Mummy! Mummy! Granny's got a snake in her stocking!'

———

We were attending my grandson's nativity play. The angelic little boy playing Joseph had been perfect until the end, when all the children assembled on stage to sing the final number, 'The Little Drummer Boy'. Three boys stood immediately behind Joseph with large drums, which they proceeded to bang with great gusto. I could see little Joseph getting increasingly agitated by the noise. Finally he turned to the drummers and exclaimed very loudly:

'Will you SHUT UP! You're doing mi 'ead in!'

———

Georgina, the granddaughter of a good friend of mine, aged about two and a half, was given a whole orange, peeled by her mother. Georgie, as she was known in the family, gazed at it with some disdain and lisped 'Thkin off.' Her mother, with commendable patience and a teacher's instinct to explain, said, 'No Georgie, mummy has taken the skin off already. That white stuff is called pith.'

Georgina's reply was succinct and wholly logical. 'Pith off,' she said sweetly.

———

Hayley, my three-year-old granddaughter, came into the bathroom just in time to see me remove my false teeth.

'Jeremy, Jeremy!' she screamed to her brother. 'Come quickly, nana is doing magic.'

———

Four similar-aged elderly ladies were guests at a friend's silver wedding lunch. Her three-year-old grandson burst in, then stopped in amazement. 'Daddy, daddy, come and look, there are four grandmas all together.'

———

Our granddaughter, Hannah, at the age of five, was absorbed in watching granddad shaving and removing his dentures, astonished to see he had 'toy teeth'.

———

I tried desperately to suppress my laughter when a child in my class informed me that his baby brother was to go into hospital to 'have an operation on his willy'. He continued that he was 'to have it circus sized'.

———

Child (very loudly) to parent, as the train sped through Doncaster Station: 'That virgin can't half shift.'

—

Overheard in the playground during the build-up to a school inspection: 'We've got to be good next week and work hard. Those "Odd Egg Inspectors" will be in school watching us.'

—

I was out walking with my five-year-old granddaughter Lucy. It was a perfect day – sunny with a beautiful blue sky.

'Isn't it a lovely sky,' said Lucy. 'But I wonder what it's like in heaven?'

'I don't know,' I said.

'No,' she replied, 'but it won't be long before you find out, will it?'

'Why has daddy got a pocket in his underpants?'

Those Tricky Questions

A teacher in a junior school was stressing the importance of safety in the home, in school and on the streets, and the children in her class were sharing their experiences. I was sitting in on the lesson.

'David, what about your accident?' asked the teacher, looking at a small boy near the front.

'Miss, I swallowed a marble,' said the boy.

'Good gracious!' exclaimed the teacher. 'That was a very silly thing to do and could have been very dangerous. You could have choked to death, couldn't he, Mr Phinn?'

'Yes, indeed,' I said.

'Miss, I was pretending it was a sweet,' continued the boy,

'and I popped it in my mouth and swallowed it by mistake. I started to cough and my mum had to smash me on the back really really hard and -'

'I think a better phrase to use would be "strike firmly" or "slap heavily", David,' interrupted the teacher.

'So, my mum had to strike me firmly on the back but it wouldn't come up, so I had to go to hospital. The doctor gave my mum this paper to get some medicine...'

'Prescription,' interposed the teacher.

'... gave mum this prescription to get some medicine and it was thick and pink and was really gross and —'

'Tasted unpleasant,' prompted the teacher.

'And it came in a big brown bottle and I had to take it for a couple of days and then one morning I was sitting on the toilet and there was a clunk and I shouted down the stairs "I've got my marble back!" and my dad said "Leave it alone!" and –'

'My goodness, David,' said the teacher hurriedly, 'what a to-do. I think we've heard quite enough about your unfortunate accident, haven't we, Mr Phinn?'

'Yes,' I said, wishing that the teacher would not constantly keep referring to me for an opinion...

I Only Asked

On Sunday, Dominic asked his dad:
'Which is the brightest star?'
'Ask your mum,' his dad replied,
'I have to clear the car.'

On Monday Dominic asked his mum:
'What's a carburettor?'
'Ask your dad,' his mum replied,
'I have to post this letter.'

On Tuesday Dominic asked his dad:
'What's a UFO?'
'Ask your mum,' his dad replied,
'The grass, it needs a mow.'

On Wednesday Dominic asked his mum:
'Which is the deepest sea?'
'Ask your dad,' his mum replied,
'I'm busy making the tea.'

On Thursday Dominic asked his dad:
'How tall are kangaroos?'
'Ask your mum,' his dad replied,
'I'm listening to the news.'

On Friday Dominic asked his mum:
'Do all kings have a crown?'
'Ask your dad,' his mum replied,
'I'm going into town.'

On Saturday Dominic asked them both:
'Do you mind me asking things,
About stars and cars and life on Mars
And kangaroos and kings?'

'Of course we don't,' his dad replied,
'Ask questions as you grow.'
'By asking things,' his mother cried,
That's how you get to know.'
Little Dominic stretched his head,
And simply answered, 'Oh.'

Six-year-old James was so excited as he had been chosen to take part in the school nativity play.

'Why can't we have Christmas every day?' he asked.

—

Four-year-old Sarah asked this question from the back of the car: 'Mummy, why are there more idiots on the road when daddy's driving?'

—

69

The new neighbours had moved in, and very soon there was a knock on the door and there stood a little girl with her bicycle.

'Have you any children?' she asked my seventy-five-year-old husband.

'I have but they've gone away,' I told her.

'Why?' she asked. 'Didn't they like you?'

—

Coming from church on Sunday, four-year-old Mark asked me: 'Mum, why does the vicar get dressed up and tell lies?'

'I don't think he does, love,' I replied.

'Oh, he does every week.'

'Why do you think that the vicar tells lies?' I asked bemused.

'Well, every Sunday he gets dressed up with his cape, puts out his hands and says "The Lord is here." Well, I've never see Him.'

—

When I was five I watched in amazement one day as grandma took out her teeth to clean them. Leaning further through the bathroom door I whispered, 'You won't be taking your eyes out, will you grandma?'

—

My young daughter was helping me hang the washing on the line when she asked: 'Mummy, why has daddy got a pocket in his underpants?'

—

'Granddad,' asked three-year-old Paul, staring at my husband's bald and shiny pate, 'how old were you when your hair slipped?'

—

When he was a youngster, my son Richard (now aged thirty and a successful accountant) was constantly asking questions: 'Why are holes empty?' 'Why are bananas bent?' 'What is the point of toes?' 'Why are oranges orange?' 'Are stars hot?' The questions were endless and I attempted to answer them as best I could. Then came the day when he asked me, 'How do people make babies?'

'I'll get your father,' I told him.

———

When my son was a toddler with enough language to start asking probing questions, he suddenly said one day, 'When I was born, did you pull my pants down to see if I was a boy or a girl?'

———

My daughter, her husband and their two little girls were having a short holiday with us. They had been out for a Sunday morning drive and unfortunately were late getting home for lunch, which was unacceptable for grandma. Halfway through lunch one of the girls said, 'Mummy, when will we be going in the doghouse?'

'I know why we have Christmas — to Sellotape Jesus'

Getting to Grips with the Language

I was just about to enter the main door of an infant school when a very distressed-looking little girl of about five or six, her face wet with weeping and her cheeks smeared where little hands had tried to wipe away the tears, tugged at my jacket.

'They've all got big sticks,' she wailed piteously.

'Who's got big sticks?' I asked, surprised.

'All on 'em. They've all got big sticks!'

'Well, they shouldn't have big sticks,' I replied.

'I want a big stick,' she cried, sniffing and sobbing, her little body shaking in anguish.

'No, you can't have a big stick. It's very dangerous,' I told her.

'I want a big stick,' she cried. 'I want a big stick.'

'You could hurt somebody with a big stick,' I said.

'But they've all got big sticks,' she howled again. 'They've all got 'em.'

At this point the headteacher appeared from the direction of the playground.

'Whatever is it, Maxine?' she asked, gently pulling the little body towards her like a hen might comfort a chick. She then looked at me. 'It's Mr Phinn, the school inspector, isn't it?'

'Yes,' I replied.

'I'm relieved about that. We have to be so careful these days. The playground supervisor came rushing into the school saying there was a strange man talking to the children.'

I suddenly felt acutely embarrassed.

'Of course, I'm so sorry. I should have come directly to the school office. It's just that this little girl was so distressed and came running up to me.' The child in question was nuzzling up to the teacher, sniffling and snuffling softly.

The small child continued to clutch the headteacher, and began to moan and groan again pitifully. 'I want a big stick, miss,' she moaned. 'They've all got big sticks.'

'Of course, you can have one,' the headteacher replied, wiping away the little girl's tears. 'You weren't there when I gave everybody one. You don't think I'd leave you out, Maxine, do you? You come with me and I'll get you a nice big one. How about that? I won't be a moment, Mr Phinn.'

'A big stick?' I murmured. 'You're giving this little girl a big stick?'

The headteacher gave a huge grin before replying, 'She means a biscuit.'

Lizzie's Road

Little Lizzie drew a long, long road
That curled across the paper like a strange, exotic snake.
She decorated it in darkest reds and brightest blues,
Gleaming golds and glittering greens.
Mum asked, 'Why all these wonderful colours?'
'Those are the rubies and emeralds and pearls,'
Lizzie explained.
'The diamonds and opals and precious stones.'
'What a wonderful road,' said mum. 'Is it magic?'
'No,' explained the child, 'It's just a jewel carriageway.'

My granddaughter, a pupil at a Roman Catholic primary school, informed me that she had been 'learning about the Immaculate Contraption'.

———

In my final year at junior school, the class of eleven year olds gave a very ambitious shadow-puppet performance to parents based on the 'Willow Pattern Plate Story'. The tension was building up in the script and the excitement grew as we reached the part where the young couple were preparing 'to flee'. The narrator, in her over-enthusiasm, inadvertently read the script as, 'Even as we speak the young couple are preparing toffee'.

———

fun

My two-and-a-half year old daughter, Jane, was being carried on her father's shoulders through Sheffield meat market when we passed a meat stall. On it was a rabbit, complete with fur, which was gutted down the front.

Jane exclaimed: 'Oh look, daddy – a pussy undone.'

———

A pupil, asked to explain the meanings of certain words, wrote: 'Erudite is a kind of glue.'

———

'Why didn't they have clothes for the baby Jesus, mummy?'

'Oh, they did. There were some lovely things to wrap him up in.'

'No there weren't, because we've learnt at school he was in a manger rude and bare.'

———

When we lived in America my daughter, Carole, aged four, attended the pre-school. Picking her up one day, I asked if she had been doing anything interesting in class that day. She told me she had learnt a new poem.

'Oh and what was that?' I asked.

'I'm a pleasant nuisance to the flag of America,' she replied.

She had been learning the Pledge of Allegiance.

———

After my four-year-old daughter had been at school for a week, I asked her how she liked being at big school.

'It's good but I haven't had my Bounty Bar yet,' she replied. I asked her what she meant and she explained: 'Well, every day before dinner, sir says, "We thank you Lord for our bounty" but nobody has given me mine yet.'

———

Whilst perusing the menu of the Chinese take-away, seven-year-old Anna announced: 'I'd like atomic crispy duck, please.'

—

On being asked to describe any pets they had, one child wrote, 'We have a dog at home. It is a library door.'

—

Discussing different types of animals, I asked the children what we call an animal that sleeps all day and comes out at night, the word beginning with the letter 'N'.

'Knackered,' came a reply.

—

Natasha, aged five, came home from school and announced to her daddy, 'Daddy, Emma weed in class today.'

'Oh dear,' replied her daddy. 'Did she have an accident?'

'No,' said Emma very indignantly, 'she weed a book.'

—

I tried to explain that at Christmas we celebrate the birthday of Jesus, and we only celebrate birthdays once a year.

A few days later one of his teachers told me James had been misleading her pupils. She explained that, the day after my conversation with James, he had arrived at school full of himself.

'Miss, miss, I know why we have Christmas – to Sellotape Jesus.'

—

The small boy told his teacher: 'My mummy and daddy were both students at university and they fell in love at the degradation ball.'

—

80

A class of six year olds had been discussing how vital water is, and how to reduce wastage. This led on to toilets and Peter piped up, "My granddad served in the sewers." The teacher thought this sounded like a good idea for a class visit or a talk to the class, so she asked his mum, who was mystified. She then realized that his granddad had been called up in 1956 and served in the Suez crisis.

———

I had been reading the story of the Nativity to an infant class, and was asking questions afterwards. 'Now class, what job had Joseph?' I asked.

One child put his hand up immediately: 'Miss, he did what my dad does. He's a carpet-fitter.'

———

Children in class were asked if anyone knew what a young rabbit was called. Bobby piped up, 'Is it a bunion?'

———

Alexander announced he had 'lost his sweating shirt' after taking it off in the playground because he was too hot. He also said, when he had a cold, that 'My nose is all blocked up and I keep bless-you-ing'.

———

My son rang me one day to ask if I could do some babysitting. Our four-year-old grandson was listening to the conversation and he called out, 'I'm not a baby, and I don't want to be sitted on.'

———

When I explained to an eight year old in my class, who complained of a headache, that teachers were not allowed to give children aspirin, he thought for a moment and asked: 'Then can I have a paramedic please?'

—

Question: 'Julia, what does "minus" mean?'
Answer: 'It's them what's on strike, sir.'

—

I was listening to my grandson read a non-fiction book about dinosaurs and was explaining what the contents and the bibliography were for.

'Do you know what a glossary is, Damien?' I asked.

'Of course, granny, it's something shiny,' he replied.

—

A number of years ago when we used to have prayers in morning assembly, my nephew came home one day and asked his mum, 'Why do we say "old men" after our prayers?'

—

I asked my six-year-old granddaughter if she knew where her funny bone was.

'My teacher says,' she replied pertly, 'that a better word than funny to use is hilarious.'

—

When my children were young, one of them came to me with a broken toy and asked me to repair it. He said, 'Please mend my car. It has come from together.'

—

'There are five books in the Old Testament,' wrote a candidate in the RE examination, 'and the first begins with Guinness.'

—

friendly

Some years ago a small member of our family, aged five, could hardly wait to go to school. When she did, she loved it. When she heard they were going to 'break up' the school she was devastated. He mother consoled her and explained they were only 'breaking up' for a half-term holiday.

———

'And what position does your father play in the football team, Andrew?' asked an infant teacher. 'He plays drawback,' the child replied.

———

At the village Harvest Festival, my class were to sing 'The Lord of the Dance'. I had carefully chosen some children to sing individually the main lines and the rest of the class were to join in the chorus. All went well until it came to Gillian's turn. She was six years old and had a beautifully loud, clear voice. Just before our turn started, I asked them if they all knew the words. Gillian looked doubtful, so I printed them out for her on a piece of paper. She was to sing 'I was cold, I was naked, were you there, were you there?' I could see her looking at the paper, and she turned, smiled at me and sang in that lovely voice: 'I was cold, I was knackered, were you there, were you there?'

———

'My granny has had go to into hospital for an operation,' the small girl told her teacher, 'because she's misplaced her hip.'

———

'My daddy came in late last night,' the small boy told his teacher. 'My mum said he was as drunk as a skunk, and this morning he has a gangover.'

———

Carol, my three-year-old daughter, began crying in the middle of the night. I went to investigate and found her holding her hand over one ear, indicating that she was in a great deal of pain. She looked up at me and said, 'Mummy, I've got dire ear.'

—

'We're doing a play at school,' my daughter announced. 'I'm playing a rabbit and Daisy is playing the main part.'

'That's nice,' I told. 'What part is Daisy playing?' I asked.

'Alison.'

'I don't think I know that play,' I said.

'Course you do mummy,' replied Rebecca. 'It's Alison Wonderland.'

—

My four-year-old daughter Suzanne was in the car with me when I collected my other daughter Wendy from secondary school.

'What have you been up to today sweetheart?' I asked Wendy.

'I'm not telling in front of big ears,' Wendy said.

'Why can't I know? I always tell you what I do at school,' said Suzanne.

'Let's have a truce until after tea shall we?' I said as I got out of the car to go to the shops. As I got back into the car a few minutes later, Suzanne said: 'I know what Wendy learned in class today, mum'.

'Oh, really?'

'Yes, she's been talking about Queen Victoria's vagina.'

As I narrowly avoided crashing the car, Wendy shouted: 'I said Queen Victoria regina!'

—

'Girls should get married and boys shouldn't'

Love and Marriage

Despite his background, Barry was a remarkably cheerful little boy who never complained and always tried his limited best at his schoolwork.

He loved nothing better than straightening the chairs, collecting the books and tidying up the classroom. He took on all these tasks cheerfully, whistling away as if he hadn't a care in the world.

Barry's teacher was to get married over the Easter holiday and, before the last lesson of the term, the children in her class presented her with presents and cards, bunches of daffodils, tulips and other spring flowers.

Barry held back until the last. He was carrying two small branches of faded broom which had seen better days and a couple of forlorn irises, wrapped in a piece of colourful paper torn out of a magazine.

'I don't want you getting married. I don't want you to,' he told his teacher. 'I don't, I don't!' And he burst into tears.

'I'll still be the same person, Barry,' his teacher assured him. 'I won't be any different.'

'You will! You will!' he wailed piteously. 'I know you will.' Then he looked up, sniffing and rubbing his eyes. 'I wanted to marry you.'

The teacher wrapped her arms around his small, shaking body. 'And are these lovely flowers for me?' she asked.

'Yes, miss,' murmured the child.

'They're beautiful – these shall be my very special flowers.' Then she whispered: 'Thank you so much, Barry. I like them better than any other flowers I have been given.'

First Love

Kimberley Bloomer wore sensible shoes
And a bright pink cardigan and snow-white socks.
Her hair was gathered in bunches and tied with red ribbons.
When she stared at me with those big blue eyes
I went wobbly at the knees.

Kimberley Bloomer was the best reader in the class.
Her voice was as soft as the summer night
And her smile made me tremble.
I sat next to her for two days,
And she smelt of flowers and lavender soap.

Kimberley Bloomer helped me with my writing.
I remember her long fingers
With nails like pink seashells.
When I got things wrong she sighed,
And I felt funny deep inside.

Kimberley Bloomer moved away.
I never saw her again.
All year I ached for Kimberley Bloomer.

When asked by my small grandson why I have been married to grandpa for over fifty years, I told him that I loved grandpa and that he loved me, and that a long time ago we fell in love. Jack sighed. 'You know granny, I don't think I'm going to bother with this falling in love. It's like learning to do number work. It's too hard and it takes too long.'

———

I was giving my teenage granddaughter a bit of advice about boyfriends. 'Looks aren't everything, Debbie, you know.' I told her. 'Just so long as he's kind.'

'Oh, I know that, granny,' she replied. 'I'm looking for a boy who is kind of rich.'

———

There was a particularly graphic sex scene on the television when Toby, my eight-year-old grandson, came down to kiss me goodnight. I quickly reached for the set and turned it off. His sharp eyes had seen what had been on the screen. 'You really don't need to do that, granny,' he told me seriously. 'I'm not interested in that sort of thing just yet.'

———

At my cousin's wedding, one of the small bridesmaids asked the bride: 'After you've got married, will you have children?'

'I expect so,' replied the bride, smiling.

'And then will you get divorced?'

———

Nine year old to grandpa: 'I'm not rushing into getting married when I grow up. I'm finding school hard enough to cope with at the moment.'

———

'Before you get married,' announced my grandson Oliver, aged six, to his little friend, 'you should practise kissing. Girls like that sort of thing.'

———

Sebastian, my great-grandson, aged seven, was attending our diamond wedding celebration held at a hotel. Many of the speeches mentioned what a remarkable achievement it was for my husband and I to have been married for so many years.

Later Sebastian sidled up. 'I suppose you must have got a bit tired living with grandpa after all that time,' he remarked.

———

Joshua complained to me that 'the girls at school keep trying to kiss me in the playground. They chase me round and I don't like it.' Then he concluded: 'I think it must be something to do with the soap I use.'

———

'I'll never kiss a girl,' said my grandson Peter, aged nine, 'because if you do you have to marry her and have babies, and I'm too young for all that sort of thing.'

———

'All the girls in my class want to go out with me,' said my grandson Matthew, aged ten.

'Really?' I replied, very amused.

'I suppose it's one of the problems with being so handsome, granny.' He gave a heaving sigh. 'And I shall just have to put up with it.'

———

One morning at the breakfast table, my son shared his wisdom with us: 'Being in love is telling your wife that she looks really pretty when she doesn't.'

———

Our young daughters were discussing their futures, and the subject of weddings came up.

The elder said, 'And I'll be all in white from head to foot.'

The younger said, 'Oh, but you can't do that. You have to have "something blue".'

Her sister replied, 'That's no problem. I shall be wearing my navy-blue gym knickers. You know how comfy they are.'

———

My son John, aged eight, was in a philosophic mood. 'You know I think girls should get married and boys shouldn't,' he told me when we were at the shops. 'Girls like soppy things like dolls and babies, and cooking and cleaning up after people, and they don't like football.'

———

My niece, aged six, a bridesmaid at my sister's wedding, was interested in what the vicar had to say at the nuptial service. She proudly announced later at the reception that she knew another name for marriage. 'It's called holy acrimony,' she announced.

———

'Polygamy is when you have more than one wife,' wrote my grandson in his homework book. 'Monotony is when you only have the one.'

———

The seventh commandment, according to my grandson, is: 'Thou shalt not admit adultery'.

Postscript

When our eldest son Richard informed us he had asked Nina to marry him, my wife and I were over the moon. I was asked to compose a special poem for their wedding – something heartfelt and poignant and, of course, I was only too pleased to oblige. I am sure that many readers will identify with the sentiments which I here express.

When I am Old!

When I'm old and I'm wrinkly, I shall not live alone
In a pensioner's flat or an old people's home,
Or take an apartment on some distant shore.
I'll move in with my son and my daughter-in-law.

I'll return all the joy that my son gave to me
When he sat as a child on his dear father's knee.
He will welcome me willingly into his home
When I'm old and I'm wrinkly and all on my own.

I'll spill coffee on the carpet, leave marks on the wall,
I'll stagger home drunk and be sick in the hall.
I'll sing really loudly and slam every door,
When I live with my son and my daughter-in-law.

I'll rise from my bed in the late afternoon,
Throw the sheets on the floor and mess up my room.
I'll play ear-splitting music well into the night,
Go down for a snack and leave on every light.

I'll rest my old feet on the new leather chairs.
I'll drape dirty underwear all down the stairs,
I'll talk to my friends for hours on the phone
When I live with my son in his lovely new home.

I'll come in from the garden with mud on my shoes,
Flop on the settee for my afternoon snooze,
Expect that my tea will be ready by four
When I live my son and my daughter-in-law.

I'll leave all the dishes piled up in the sink
And invite all my noisy friends round for a drink,
I'll grumble and mumble, I'll complain and I'll moan
When I'm old and I'm wrinkly and all on my own.

I'll watch television hour after hour,
I'll not flush the toilet or wash out the shower
Oh, bliss, what a future for me is in store
When I move in with my son and my daughter-in-law.

Little Gems
Gervase Phinn

Dalesman

First published in Great Britain 2004
by Dalesman
an imprint of
Country Publications Ltd
The Water Mill, Broughton Hall,
Skipton North Yorkshire BD23 3AG
www.dalesman.co.uk

Reprinted 2004 (twice), 2005 (twice), 2006, 2007, 2008

A British Library Cataloguing-in-Publication record
is available for this book.

ISBN: 978-1-85568-212-2

Designed by Butler & Tanner Ltd
Colour origination by PPS Grasmere Ltd
Printed and bound in China

PUBLISHER'S NOTE
The Publishers express its gratitude to the children whose poems,
stories and illustrations are reproduced in this book. Copyright is expressly
reserved on their behalf. However, given the nature of the material, it has not
been possible, despite every effort by Gervase Phinn and Country Publications Ltd,
to contact every contributor. In lieu of copyright fees, Country Publications Ltd has
made a donation to the British Dyslexia Association.

CONTENTS

Introduction

One delightful and unexpected result of the publication of my autobiographical accounts about my time as school inspector in the Yorkshire Dales is the phenomenal amount of mail I have received. Interested readers have entertained me with letters, cards, anecdotes, poems and little stories about what their children and grandchildren have said. Some were witty, others hilarious and a few were deeply poignant.

Robert Flanagan, director of Dalesman Publishing, suggested that I might like to let others share in my enjoyment of the pieces and further suggested that we ask readers of *Dalesman* magazine to submit their own 'little gems' to add to the collection. Hence this anthology, which I hope you will enjoy reading as much as I have compiling.

I am very grateful for all those who took the time and trouble to send me so much wonderful material. It has not always been possible to trace the author of every piece, so I extend my thanks to all those who contributed anonymously. Sadly, I cannot publish all the 'little gems' because there were so many; I have had to settle for selecting my special favourites.

Acknowledgements

Thanks go to the pupils and staff of the following schools for their help in providing illustrations: Leamington Primary and Nursery School, Sutton-in-Ashfield; All Saints C E Primary School, Aston; Holy Trinity C E (Aided) Primary School, Leeds; Follifoot C E Primary School, Harrogate; Hookstone Chase Primary School, Harrogate; Wilmslow Preparatory School, Cheshire; Christ the King R C Primary School, Thornaby, Stockton-on-Tees; Polam Hall Junior School, Darlington; St Mary Magdelene R C Primary School, Milton Keynes.

The following *Dalesman* readers have kindly contributed to the text: Tony Atkins; E E Avill; Geoff Beecroft; Mr R Billups; Harold Blackburn; Margaret Bottomley; Dorothy Brown; Mrs R E Brown; Don Bullough; Pat Burke; Reginald P Burn; Mrs P Carroll; Betty Charlesworth; Joyce Clarke; Miss E Clarkson; Marilyn Connors; Barbara Cottiswood; Vicky Crossfield; Mrs Dorothy Croxford; Mrs B Cunliffe; Marian Deeds; Ian Denison; Irene Dick; Barbara Dobson; Mrs B Eddon; John Evans; Meg Fellows; Colin Fletcher; Elsie M Fletcher; Mrs Muriel Fryatt; Mrs F M Garth; H Goodall; Anne Gordon; F P Hargreaves; H W Higginbottom; E Holmes;

Glenys Hughes; Jean Hughes; Marcia Hunt; Daphne Ibbott; Mrs J S Ibbotson; Dorothy Jackson; Jane Jackson; Wm A Jagger; Mrs L Johnson; Doris Lomax; Mrs D Lord; Penny Marfleet; John Marsden; Mrs J McCormack; Mrs Irene Meggison; Edith Morgan; Mrs M Muirhead; Harry Myers; Georgina Newton; Gillian Osborn; Brenda Parker; Barbara Payne; Morris Pearson; Mrs M Peason; Bruce Poll; Ernest Pollard; Shirley Ramsey; Nora Riley; Marie Robinson; Hugh Rowland; Mrs C M Sadler; Mrs Marian Samme; Pauline and Geoff Schofield; Mary and Bryan Shackleton; D H Shepherd; Anita Simcox; Mrs P Slater; Mr & Mrs Roy Smart; Moira Smith; R G Smith; Sally Smith; Connie Staples; Joan Stephenson; David Sumner; Elspeth Tanner; Mavis Thomas; Edward Thompson; Mrs D Thompson; Joan Thompson; Mrs M Thompson; Anne Thorpe; Miss Margaret Thorp; Miss A Townson; Mrs J M Waller; Mary Walsh; Yvonne Warburton; Edna Ward; John Ward; Connie Waters; Mrs Janice M Watson; Rosemary Wells; Bernard Wilkinson; Marian Williams; Meg Williams; Betty Wilson; Margaret Wilson; Barbara Winkfield; Neville Withers; Mrs Anne P Wood.

That's no lady, that's my Grandma

Grannies and Grandpas

The relationship between grandparents and their grand-children is rather different from that between parents and their children. Grannies and grandpas, in my experience, tend to be more patient, better listeners, less critical and, dare I say it, more indulgent than their own offspring.

It was the weekly ritual for my mother, well into her eighties, to come around for Sunday lunch. From her vantage point in the most comfortable chair in the corner of the sitting room, she would watch as my wife Christine and I attempted to bring up our four children. One Sunday I had occasion to chastise Matthew, then aged six, for his untidy bedroom. Stabbing the air with a finger, I ordered him: 'Up those stairs now, young man, and tidy your bedroom! Do you follow my drift?' Matthew at first looked suitably contrite but then a small smile appeared on his lips, then a grin to be followed by giggles and finally guffaws. I ballooned with anger. Then I caught sight of my mother in the mirror. She was sitting behind me pulling the most ridiculous faces and wiggling her fingers in front of her nose.

'Mother!' I snapped rather pompously. 'I am trying to instil some discipline here. You are not helping matters!'

'Oh, do be quiet,' she told me. 'You're not talking to teachers now.'

'Mother ...!' I began.

'Don't mother me. He's a lovely little boy is Matthew. He's kind, compassionate, gentle and well behaved. You should be telling him that, not hectoring him. Goodness me, there are more important things in life than an untidy room and yours was like a tip when you were a boy.'

Father and son were stuck for words.

She continued. 'I don't suppose I should tell your daddy off in front of you, Matthew,' she said, 'but he's wrong.' Then she gave me a knowing look and one of her smiles, and added 'And he's my little boy'.

Having read this account, you will understand why the poem which begins this section on grannies and grandpas has a particular resonance for me.

My Nan

I like my Nan.
She's round and wrinkly and powdery
And smells of flowers and soap.
She's as comfy as a cushion to sit on.
When my Mum shouts at me
I go to my Nan.
She cuddles me and says,
'Never mind love,
Your Mum was like that
When she was a little girl –
A real grumpybum!'

Mark (aged nine)

At our granddaughter's third birthday party, I was taking photographs when one little boy chimed up: 'Jamie Lee, that lady is taking your picture.'

'That's no lady!' said my granddaughter. 'That's my grandma!'

———

A week prior to Christmas, I was shopping with my small grandson in a supermarket. As we passed a freezer, I asked him: 'Why do you think that freezer is full of frozen turkeys?'

'To make sure they're dead,' he replied.

———

Granddaughter asking her rather diminutive grandfather:

'Granddad, why are you so small for your age?'

My Grandma

I loved my Grandma
She was very thoutfull
Her hair was like silver
And her face like gold
Eyes like emerolds
That glinted in the sun.
She was very preicious.

My Grandma

I loved my Grandma.
She was very thoughtful.
Her hair was like silver
And her face like gold,
Eyes like emeralds
That glinted in the sun.
She was very precious.

Amy (aged six)

'Grandpa, were you in the first war?'
'No, I hadn't been born.'
'Were you in the second war?'
'No, I wasn't old enough.'
Short pause for thought.
'Couldn't you go out and start one?'

—

I have seven grandsons. When reaching the age of seven I decide to take each of them to Legoland for the weekend. Michael had been and now it was Glenn's turn. His younger brother, Roger, was upset and wanted to go with him.

'Well, Roger,' I explained, 'in two years time it will be your turn to go and after you there is still Douglas, Cameron, Laurence and Jack.'

'Never mind, Grandma,' consoled Roger, 'I don't expect you will live that long.'

—

Overheard, my small grandchild and her little friend in deep conversation: 'Well, my Daddy says my Grannie's past her sell-by date.'

—

'Grannie,' said Bethany, aged five, 'I know the "F" word.'
'Oh dear!' I said in mock horror, 'you must never say it.'
'I don't, Grannie,' she replied. 'I say trump.'

My Granddad

He is bald my granddad is,
Got no hair at all.
Lots of crinklies round his eyes
And on his cheeks as well.
He laughs at me and Natalie.
His face goes all funny.
Makes wrinkles on his face
Like lots of lines
On my trousers.

Luke (aged six)

Grandson to grandfather: 'Who'll get the fish and chips when you've gone to heaven?'

—

I was at my dressing table, putting some lipstick on and getting ready to go to a WI meeting. My granddaughter, Amy, aged six, was combing my hair.

'Can't find any nits yet, Grannie,' she told me.

Dalesman Grandfather

Old man, smoky beard,
Sunshine smile and haystack hair,
Hands like roots and corn gold skin,
He doesn't have a single care.

Old man, falcon nosed,
Bent old back and raven's eye,
Thin as a scarecrow in his fields,
He stands and sees the world go by.

Daniel (aged ten)

A little Gunnerside tot was looked after by both grans but spent a lot of time with her Dales grannie. On being complimented on her new cardigan by the 'off com'd un' grandmother, little Ruth tugged at the sleeve, grimaced and said, 'Ee, there's no body in this – it won't last five minutes!'

—

Grandson: 'Granddad, we've been asked to take something very very old into school. Will you come in with me tomorrow?'

—

Zachary, my great-nephew, all of seven years old, was upset to hear that his granddad had undergone open heart surgery. On a visit to the hospital he informed his parents seriously that he had decided what he was going to say to his granddad when he saw him: 'Granddad, I love you very much – but with a tinge of sadness.'

My Granny

My Grannie says I am a little chatterbox.
She says I talk ten to the dozen.

Chatter chatter, chatter.
Natter, natter, natter.

My Grandpa says, 'Never mind poppet.
You take after your grannie.

Chatter chatter, chatter.
Natter, natter, natter.

She's the world champion talker.'

Elizabeth (aged six)

I'm eighty-two years old and was having an afternoon snooze on the settee when in comes my granddaughter. 'Wake up, Granddad,' she ordered, 'this is my new friend, Michael. He hasn't got a granddad and I've brought him in to show him what one looks like.'

—

My great-granddaughter, Ruth Hannah, aged five, informed me: 'Gramps, you have got a beard.'

'No, Ruth, I have a shave every morning.'

'Yes, you have. It's up your nose.'

Grandpa

My Grandpa is old now.
His head is as bald as a hard-boiled egg
But inside millions of things are going on.

My Grandpa is old now,
But when he sneezes
He blows the leaves off the trees.

My Grandpa is old now,
But when he walks
His legs go snip-snap like a pair of scissors.

My Grandpa is old now,
But when he smiles
The sun comes out and the birds sing.

My Grandpa is old now.
But he doesn't act his age.

Elizabeth (aged seven)

I explained to my grandson, aged five, who had asked where my dog was, that Rusty was very old and tired and had had a long and happy life and that the vet had 'put him to sleep.'

'When will you be going to the vet then, Grandma?' he asked.

—

At lunch, my small grandson asked casually: 'Granddad, can I have this house when you pop your clogs?'

—

Whilst recovering from a cataract operation I asked my granddaughter to pick up her toys, explaining that I couldn't bend down yet. 'Why? Will your eye fall out, Gran?' she asked.

—

I am a very careful driver, if a little on the slow side. I was taking my small grandson, Harry, aged six, to a birthday party and we were running rather late. As I trundled along the road, he gave a great heaving sigh and said in a very exasperated tone of voice: 'Step on it Gran, for God's sake. We'll be here all day at this rate.'

On another occasion I nearly crashed the car because of my uncontrollable laughter. Harry, strapped in the back, watched fascinated as an impatient young driver overtaking me after a road junction, made a very rude sign in my direction.

'Grannie,' Harry said cheerfully, 'I think the man in the car in front is showing you his poorly finger.'

—

Hayley, my three-year-old granddaughter, came into the bathroom just in time to see me remove my false teeth.

'Jeremy! Jeremy!' she screamed to her brother. 'Come quickly, Nana is doing magic!'

—

Four-year-old granddaughter staring intently at her granddad's bald pate: 'Granddad, you haven't been eating your crusts.'

—

22

When I was honorary curator of the Manor House Museum, Ilkley, I encouraged children to bring finds, always hoping something of importance would turn up. In came a little girl with three stones in her hand.

'What are these, dear?' I asked.

'My granny's gallstones,' was the smiling reply.

———

My granddaughter, Sydney, when she was four, decided to comb everyone's hair. When she got to me, she ran the comb gently up and down and then stopped, sat back and remarked: 'Papa, you might have lots of wrinkles but you have the most handsome hair.'

———

Grandson was visiting grandma for the day. Grandma said: 'You have got a bad cough.'

His reply was: 'I've got one at home as well.'

———

Granddad, collecting his small granddaughter from school, asked her to take her school bag and coat out to the car. 'You're not too old to carry things yourself, granddad, you know,' she replied pertly.

———

A niece, now in her sixties, had a grandfather who had very large ears. One day she said to her mother, 'When Grandpa dies will he become an angel?'

The mother replied, 'I expect so, dear, why do you ask?'

'Oh, I thought he'd become an elf,' replied the child.

———

My granddaughter, aged six, came into the bathroom where I was quietly removing, with the aid of tweezers, an odd whisker on my chin.

'Grandma,' she said, 'I will be glad when I am old and have hairs on my face.'

—

Felicity, aged three, asked me why she hadn't got a granddad. I explained to her that he had gone to Heaven.

'I suppose you'll be next,' said Felicity in a matter-of-fact little voice.

'There is great-grandma,' I reminded her.

'Yes, but she doesn't go anywhere by herself,' replied the child.

—

My granddaughter Jessica was watching in fascination as I cleaned my false teeth in the bathroom. I explained that, unlike hers, mine weren't real and I take them out to wash them to keep them nice and fresh. She noticed a bar of Pears soap on the washbasin – the round, brown, transparent kind. 'Is that your tongue, Grannie?' she asked.

COD

Mummy, what does God stand on?

God, religion and going to church

When it comes to God and religion, young children are immensely disarming, and their questions and observations frequently leave the adult lost for words.

On a visit to a school deep in the Yorkshire Dales, I observed the school assembly taken by a very genial vicar. He started his assembly by asking the children to try and guess what was in his head. He told them that, as he had walked through the churchyard on his way to the school that morning, he had seen something behind a tree. It had been grey and hairy with a great bushy tail and little darting, black, shiny eyes like beads.

'And what do you think I'm talking about?' he had asked the children.

A large, ruddy-complexioned boy with a mop of very fair hair replied: 'I know it's Jesus, vicar, but it sounds like a squirrel to me.'

On another occasion, a young and very enthusiastic curate read, from a large crimson-covered children's Bible, the parable of 'The Good Samaritan' and explained to his young audience how the story taught us all how to lead better lives. He could see by the fidgeting and turning of heads that it was not having a massive impact, so he decided to finish. But not before posing one final question.

'And what would you say to Jesus,' he asked, holding high the red book like some preacher of old, 'if He were to walk into the hall this morning?'

The boy on the front row thought for a moment, then raised his hand and said loudly, 'I'd give 'im that there book, vicar, and I'd say, "Jesus Christ – this is your life".'

I fared little better in an assembly that I took. I related the parable on 'The Lost Sheep' and asked the children the question: 'Why do you think the shepherd risked losing all his other sheep just for the one which was lost?', and some bright spark replied, ''Appen it were t' tup.'

Many of the 'little gems' in this section bring a smile to the lips, but the first poem I find extremely affecting coming, as it does, from one so young.

God

When I was little,
I thought that God
Was like Captain Birdseye
Without the fish fingers.
I thought that God
Always smiled and had a friendly face,
That he was tall and kind
And never shouted.
Now I am older,
I think that God
Is like an old old man
Without any children.
I think that God
Has a sad and tired face,
That he cries
And groans
To see the world
He made.

Sean (aged nine)

Child to vicar: 'Are you growing a beard to be more like Jesus?'

—

The first time our son Ian was shown the vicarage, he asked: 'Is that where they make Vick?'

God.

When I was little,
I thought that God
Was like Captain Birdseye
Without the fishfingers.
I thought that God
Allways smiled and had a friendly face,
That he was tall and kind
And never ever shouted.

Now I am older,
I think that God
Is like an old old man
Without any children.
I think that God
Has a sad and tired face,
That he cries
And groans
To see the world
He made.

Lucy's Carol

When the Baby borned
Joseph said to Mary,
'What am I going to do about
This little-born Jesus Baby Christ?
I never knew it was going to be like this,
With all these angels and kings
And shepherds and stars and things;
It's got me worried, I can tell you,
On Christmas Day in the morning.'
Mary said to Joseph,
'Not to worry darling,
Dear old darling Joseph;
Everything's going to be all right,
Because the Angel told me not to fear;
So just hold up the lamp,
So I can see the dear funny sweet little face
Of my darling Little-born Jesus Baby Christ'.
Joseph said to Mary,
'Behold the handy-man of the Lord.'
Happy Christmas, happy Christmas'
Christ is born today.

Lucy (aged four,
recorded by her mother as she talked to her dolls)

At the Christmas morning service, the last carol had been sung and there was a moment's quiet before 'the dismissal'. In the silence as we all bowed our heads in prayer, an impatient little voice echoed around the church: 'Can we go now, mummy?'

The reply from the priest was instantaneous: 'In a minute.'

—

The vicar asked the children: 'Now, what do you know about Jesus?'

My son, Joshua, aged six, replied: 'Well, I know he likes fish.'

—

On a dark, clear, starry night, grandpa took his four-year-old granddaughter into the garden for a lesson on the 'Sky at Night'.

'What do they call it up there?' she asked, staring upwards.

'That's Heaven,' explained grandpa. 'It's where all the good people go.'

'Well, if I don't like it the first time I go,' the little girl told him, 'I won't go again.'

—

Christopher, aged five, looking into the sky: 'Mummy, what does God stand on? Perhaps it's a hard cloud.'

—

A mother was teaching her little girl the Lord's Prayer, asking the child to repeat each phrase after her. One evening the little girl announced proudly that she could say it all by herself and began with great gusto. She recited the prayer perfectly until she came to the line: 'And deliver us from evil.' Instead she said proudly: 'And deliver us some e-mail.'

—

Emily, aged three, asked: 'Mummy, does Jesus tell us everything?'

'Yes,' replied her mother.

'Well, I think he's telling us to go to Toys R Us', said the child.

—

My son, in primary school, spent much time drawing. His teacher asked him about one particular sketch.

'Who is this?' she enquired.

'God,' he replied,

'No-one knows what God looks like,' she informed him.

'Well they will when they see this,' replied the child.

—

When the vicar entered the classroom, one small boy sighed 'Oh God' under his breath.

Without pausing for thought, the vicar smiled and said loudly, 'No, not God, just one of His friends.'

—

The bishop had visited my grandson's infant school, and let the children try on some of his regalia and hold his precious crosier. Following his visit, the children were asked to write and thank him. Joshua wrote: 'Thank you for coming into our school, Bishop John. I now know what a crook looks like.'

—

When my godson Oliver was asked what he would like to give up for Lent, he replied: 'School.'

—

Small child in church during an inordinately long sermon: 'Grannie, is it still Sunday?'

—

A small girl who was making her first Holy Communion seemed to be rather nervous and insisted on returning to the toilet in the church. Annie, my wife, of course allowed her to go again but did say she should have gone before coming into church. When the child appeared after her second visit she announced:

'Hasn't God got a lovely toilet?'

—

I was telling my small granddaughter about the journey of the Israelites into the wilderness and the miraculous provision of manna. On finishing the story I asked the little one what she thought manna was.

'Well, Grandpa,' she said confidently, 'you see there are good mannas and bad mannas.'

—

The vicar was addressing the infant school assembly. 'When I last saw some of you children,' he said, 'you were brought into my church as babies, all in white with your mummies and daddies, family and friends. It was a very very special occasion. Does anyone know what I did to you when you were a tiny baby and were brought to church?' The children stared wide-eyed but silent. 'Well, I will give you a clue,' continued the vicar, undeterred by the lack of response. 'The word I am thinking of begins with a curly C.' He stared at the blank faces and persevered. 'I chr …chr…chr …anyone know?'

A child shouted out: 'Crucified.'

—

At Sunday morning service, the vicar referred to a verse from the Bible: 'He that hath ears to hear, let him hear.' He then asked the children: 'And what do you do with your ears?'

In a flash a little lad raised his hand and called out: 'You wash behind them.'

—

The preacher entered the pulpit and the small door closed behind him. He proved to be rather flamboyant, waving his arms about in dramatic gestures to emphasise a point. A clear penetrating little voice of the small child echoed around the church: 'Granny, whatever will he do if he gets out?'

—

My brother John, a Roman Catholic priest, had all the small children around the altar at Mass. 'God loves us all and takes care of us,' he told the little ones. 'He's a very good listener too, so when we want to thank Him or ask Him for His help, He listens. Now children, how do we talk to God?' he asked, expecting them to respond by saying that we all say our prayers every night. He was surprised and not a little amused when one bright spark shouted: 'You could always text Him.'

—

At the rear of our church is a set of boxes and on each is a label: 'For the altar flowers', 'For the candles', 'For the missions'. My little grandson Jamie, aged six, was very keen to show me how good a reader he was and recited every label with ease. He paused at the last box and thought for moment. 'This one's useful, Granddad,' he said, 'if your tummy's feeling a bit poorly.' On the front of the box was written: 'For the sick.'

—

When the local parish priest visited our first school, one child asked him: 'Why do they call you father if you haven't any children?'

———

My little granddaughter Katherine told me she was about to make her 'First Holy Communion'.

———

My thirteen-year-old stepson was playing football with some friends in a local park when he was approached by a pair of missionaries from the evangelical church.

'What would you do if we told you that Jesus saves?' they asked.

The youngster replied: 'I'd put him in goal.'

———

At Sunday school, the young vicar asked the children what Jesus did first thing in the morning and last thing at night, something that we too should do. He, of course, was expecting: 'Say our prayers'. The reply from one little boy was: 'Go to the toilet.'

———

Young child just before we said our prayers: 'I'm sick of talking to God with my eyes closed.'

Mummy, I know a dirty word

The things children say

Smile and the young child will smile back. Little ones don't know what cynicism is; they don't know how to curl a lip and are unconcerned about skin colour, background, race, religion, accent and the things which often cause so much distress and conflict in the world.

Little children have no conception of status or rank, and judge those they meet without preconceptions. They are innately curious, open, innocent, spontaneous and honest. Sometimes, it has to be said, they are a little too honest.

Once on a school visit in York I was informed by a six-year-old child: 'Have you ever thought that when I'm twenty-one, you'll probably be dead?' On another occasion, I commented to a little boy in the infant classroom that his writing at the top of the page was lovely and neat, but went all squiggly at the bottom. 'I know,' he said sighing, 'this pen's got a life of its own.'

On a visit to a Rotherham school with the mayor to see the Christmas play, we were puzzled to notice that all the children were coming out of the building and heading for home.

'Where's everyone going?' his worshipful asked a little boy with hair like a lavatory brush and a face as speckled as hen's egg. 'We've come for the nativity.'

'Aaah, well, it's off,' the little boy informed him.

'Off?' repeated the mayor.

'Aye,' said the child. 'T' Virgin Mary's got nits.'

I recall the time during my first year as an inspector when I found a corner of an infant classroom set out as a baby clinic and a small girl clutching a large doll to her chest. She was surrounded by scales, towels, feeding bottles, a plastic bath and a toy cot.

As I approached, she looked up alarmed. 'Go away!' she cried. 'I'm breast feeding.'

So, 'Here's to the child and all he or she has to teach us', as the old Irish saying tells us. Enjoy the bluntness and honesty of the children in this section; the things they say in the small anecdotes, cameos, poems and prose pieces are guaranteed to delight.

The Owl

The bird I am going to tell you about is the owl. The owl cannot see by day and at night is as blind as a bat. I do not know anything else about an owl so I will tell you about a cow.

The cow is a mammal. It has six sides – a right, left, upper and below. At the back it has a tail on which hangs a brush. With this it sends the flies away so that they do not fall into its milk.

The head of the cow is for the purpose of growing horns on and so that the mouth can be somewhere. The horns are to butt with and the mouth is to moo with.

The legs of the cow go right down to the ground.

Under the cow hangs the milk. It has been arranged for milking. When people milk, the milk comes out and there's never an end to the supply. How the cow does this I do not know but it makes more and more. The cow has a fine sense of smell. You can smell it far away. This is the reason for the fresh air in the countryside.

The man cow is called an ox. It is not a mammal.

The cow does not eat much but what it eats it eats twice so that it always gets enough. When the cow is hungry it moos and when it says nothing it is because its insides are full of grass.

Martha (aged six)

Paul, aged three, whispered: 'Mummy, I know a dirty word.'

'Do you, Paul?' asked his shocked mother.

'Dustbin,' confided the child.

—

Paige and Jay, aged six and four respectively, were in trouble because someone had bitten a piece out of the bath sponge. Paige pleaded her innocence: 'It wasn't me honestly and that's the truth', she said.

Jay looked up at his daddy with eyes as big and as round as saucers, and said: 'It wasn't me and I am making the truth up.'

———

Miriam, aged six, on being told sadly by her mother that daddy wouldn't be able to go on holiday with them one year because he was so busy, shrugged and replied: 'I can live with that'.

———

I tried to be as sensitive and tactful as possible when my small granddaughter, Lucy, asked where my dog was. 'It was time for him to go,' I explained in a very sad and quiet voice, 'and the vet had to put him to sleep.'

'You mean he killed him,' Lucy told me.

———

Following a little accident on the hall floor during assembly, an infant explained to his teacher: 'My willy went out of control.'

———

I overheard a conversation in my local market town between two five-year-old girls:

'Sylvia, have you got that chewing-gum I lent you?'

'No, I've lost it.'

'Well, you'll have to find it, 'cos it's our Robert's.'

———

Andrew, aged four, came dashing into the house shouting: 'Mummy, Mummy, my caterpillars in the jar on the windowsill are turning into Christians.'

———

I took my five-year-old daughter to London Zoo, and we were standing in a crowd watching the chimpanzees. A very obviously male chimpanzee was lying on his back lifting a baby chimp up and down.

My daughter said, 'Oh, look at that mummy chimpanzee playing with her baby.'

Without thinking I said, 'That's not a mummy, it's a daddy.'

Quick as a flash my daughter said, 'Oh, of course it's a daddy. It's just lying around doing nothing.'

———

Four-year-old asking his father: 'Dad, you know that you said that you would never get this model railway finished? Well, the day you die, will you write down all that still needs doing and I'll finish it?'

———

My daughter, aged six, flung her arms around me, buried her nose in my tummy, breathed deeply and exclaimed, 'Oh, I do like the smell of old age.'

———

Sarah found a dead mouse. We buried it and told her that it had gone to Heaven. After a while she came to me and said: 'Grandma, shall we dig it up and see if it's gone yet?'

———

Dear Mr. Phinn,
          Please (pretty please) can you
come to officially open Hade Edge
School. Your book "Royston Knapper" is
brilliant! Well so I've heard.
          After you open our school, you
can join in with our party! I don't what's
happening about our party, because its
teachers biusness.
          And after that, you can have a
walk areuned Holmesties, our reservoir.
Smell the fresh air!
          So please come here. You need
to! Everyone else couldn't come so you
should!

The Invitation

Dear Mr Phinn,

Please (pretty please!) can you come to officially open Hade Edge School?

Your book 'Royston Knapper' is brilliant! Well so I've heard. After you open our school, you can join in with our party. I don't know what's happening about our party, because it's teachers' business. And after that you can have a walk around Holmesties, our reservoir. Smell the fresh air.

So please come here. You need to! Everyone else couldn't come so you should!

Sam Walls (aged eleven)

A Roman Soldier Writes Home

Greetings Paulinus,

It's been a bad week!

I've just got back from boring old Britain. It's cold and gloomy, wet and windy. And you should see the Britons. Ugh! Big, ugly, smelly, fat, screaming, hairy yobs.

The surroundings are horrible and Sergeant Andus is nasty to us all. I miss the sunshine and the grapes and the wine.

I will have to stop now as my spaghetti is getting cold.

Dominicus

PS I also have diarrhoea.

Dominic (aged nine)

When I was four, I was taken out to tea for the first time. A plate of exceedingly tiny sandwiches was offered to mother, with the suggestion that she should take two while the plate was there. She duly did. Then it came to my turn so I said, 'I'll take two, while I'm here, shall I?'

—

A small boy was invited out to tea by a certain Miss Somebody in the locality. During tea he suddenly addressed his hostess, saying: 'Are you called Miss because you have missed being married?'

—

My son, aged two, is beginning to talk. The other day he pointed to the half-moon and commented: 'Sunshine broken.'

Becky

Becky didn't like reading,
She didn't like singing,
She didn't like riding her bike,
She didn't like running,
She didn't like shopping,
She didn't like watching TV,
She didn't like sweets.
She was a pain in the Bum.

Laura (aged six)

Becky dident
like reading
she dident
like singing
she dident
like riding
her bike
she dident
like running
she dident
like shoping

she dident
like waching
T-V
she dident
like sweets
she was a
pain in the
Bum

One foggy day, our small grandson, after looking pensively out of the window for some time, asked: 'Gran, where's the outside gone?'

—

I asked my infant daughter if she would like an ice cream (her very first). She watched several children eating ice cream cornets, and replied: 'Yes please, Daddy, I'll have one with a handle on.'

Lost

One day my mummy and daddy went to Ripon and I went too. Daddy went in a bookshop with the brothers and mummy went in a dress shop with me. I hid in some coats. They could not find me. mummy cried and daddy panicked. The brothers stood as still as stone. After a few minutes I popped out my head and said: 'Peepo.'

'You little horror,' said mummy.

Elizabeth (aged seven)

My young daughter, when we were visiting another family, was on her very best behaviour during the main course. As we continued to chat and no move was made to bring dessert, she asked politely: 'Would you like me to have some pudding?'

—

It was a particularly appetising school dinner, but no second helpings were available. A young 'hopeful', receiving this news, sadly remarked: ' If there's ivver owt good, there's nivver nowt left.'

—

Mark, as a very young child, eyed some vegetables on his plate with grave suspicion and asked his mother what they were. She explained that they were called parsnips. He nodded. 'Is that what they sing about at Christmas time?' he asked. We looked puzzled so he explained: 'Parsnips in a pear tree?'

———

Our two-year-old daughter, in the middle of potty training, announced she wanted to go to the toilet at a very inconvenient time. Her grandma told her to wait and try to hold it. Her immediate response was: 'Nanna, I can't hold it because it hasn't got a handle.'

———

After watching my four-year-old niece drawing pictures of people with purple hair and in garish garb, using felt tip pens with reckless abandon, I became worried that she may be colour blind. Out one day on a walk, I put my fears to the test.

I said, 'If you stood in this field of rape in your yellow play-suit and if I stood by this hawthorn hedge in my dark green tweeds, noone would ever see us, would they?' She rolled her eyes upwards and said pityingly: 'Auntie, I think the word you are seeking is camouflage.'

———

Driving past a gentlemen's toilet, Jamie remarked: 'Auntie, that's where dogs come from.' Puzzled, I asked him why he thought so and he replied: 'Because every time my daddy goes in there, he says he's going to see a man about a dog.'

———

We live near a large lake and many of the frogs, on their travels along the village road, perish beneath the wheels of the traffic. Angus, aged four, looked in amazement at the many bodies which littered the road and asked, 'Auntie, why didn't they look left and right before crossing?'

—

This is a definition of a hill from my mother's remembrance of her schooldays in Bradford, seventy years ago: 'A gret lump o' muck, slantin' up straight.'

—

I am a teacher. One day shopping with my three year old, she asked, 'Mummy, can I have an ice cream, please?'

'No.'

'Well, can I have some sweeties?'

'No.'

'Well, can I have I have a biscuit?'

'No.'

'Well, I don't want another bloody book.'

—

In the 1940s, when I taught at Stetford Junior Commercial School, the entrance examination required students to put words into sentences to show their meanings. One word was 'flourish'. A bright spark wrote: 'Don't forget to flourish the toilet when you've been.'

—

My husband and I and our three sons, Jacob, Thomas and Andrew, aged twelve, nine and six, spent a weekend at a rather exclusive Scottish hotel on special offer. Children under the age of eleven went half price and my husband, being a canny

Yorkshireman, was intent on spending as little money as possible. At the reception desk the young woman asked how many of the children were under eleven.

'All of them,' my husband told her confidently.

'No, Daddy,' piped up Andrew, 'Jacob is twelve.'

'No, I'm not,' snapped his eldest brother, fully aware of his father's reasons for telling the fib and happy to collude.

'Yes, you are,' persisted Andrew, 'and stop kicking me.'

'Ah yes,' said my husband, looking decidedly embarrassed. 'He's just had his birthday.'

'No, he hasn't, Daddy,' exclaimed Andrew, 'his birthday was a long time ago. It was on May 4th.'

'Of course,' mumbled my husband. 'Silly me.' Then he smiled weakly at the very amused receptionist. 'Two children under eleven and one over,' he said sheepishly.

Later in the restaurant I reminded him of the words of Scotland's most famous poet:

'Oh what a tangled web we weave
When first we practise to deceive.'

I know the difference between girls and boys

The facts of life

How many parents have been asked that tricky question: 'Where do I come from?' Children are naturally inquisitive and very persistent when they think they are being fobbed off, given a lame excuse or told a fanciful story.

When my son Dominic was six, he asked the dreaded question: 'Daddy, where do I come from?'

'I'll get your mother,' I said quickly.

The three of us sat him down on the settee, Dominic sandwiched between my wife and me, and tried to explain to him, slowly and honestly, how he came into the world. We told him that daddy loved mummy, and mummy loved daddy, and how sometimes they had an extra-close cuddle. I could hear myself sounding more and more like Joyce Grenfell. I told him about mummy having an egg and daddy having a sperm, and the other facts of life.

'So does that explain it, Dominic?' I asked.

He stared up at me with wide unblinking eyes and sighed heavily. 'No, it doesn't,' he said. 'I just wanted to know where I come from. Andrew comes from Sheffield.'

I was once approached by a small boy in an infant school who announced bluntly: 'I know how to mek babies, you know.'

I smiled, nodded sagely, tried not to look in the least shocked and replied in a very casual voice, 'Really?'

'Aye, I do. I've just learnt how to mek babies.' There was a pregnant pause. 'Do you know how to mek babies then?' he asked.

'I do, yes,' I replied

There was another long pause. 'How do you mek babies, then?' the boy asked, looking me straight in the eye.

'You go first,' I told him.

'Well', he said, 'I knock the "y" off and add "i-e-s".'

My mother was looking after her little cousins, a boy and a girl, who were playing doctors and nurses. After a quiet period the little boy rushed into the room shouting: 'Doctor, doctor, come quick. A baby's been born and we can't find the mother.'

—

My son, aged four, on seeing my bra hanging over a chair back in the bedroom, asked: 'Is that where you keep baby's dinner, Mummy?'

—

My grandson, Callum, aged six, told me, nodding confidently and pointing downwards, 'I know the difference between girls and boys, Grannie.'

'Really,' I replied, imagining the tricky conversation which would ensue.

'It's down there, Grannie.'

'Is it?'

'Boys have bigger feet.'

—

My grandson Christopher and I were playing cricket in the back garden and it was his turn to bowl. Before he did so, he gave me the benefit of his considerable experience (he was six): 'Be very careful, Grandpa, don't let the ball hit you in the nuts. It can be very painful.'

—

I took my little grandson George, aged six, to the swimming baths. As I changed into my trunks, he pointed to a private part of my anatomy and observed: 'I've got one of those, Grandpa.'

'Yes, I know,' I said, 'all little boys have one.'

'My Daddy's got one as well.'

'Yes, I know, and all men have them too.'

'Yours is a lot bigger than mine.'

'Yours will get bigger when you get older,' I told him.

He wrinkled his little nose.

'You're older than Daddy, Grandpa, aren't you?' said George.

'That's right,' I replied.

'Well, why is Daddy's a lot bigger than yours?'

I was stumped.

—

A Yorkshire farmer's wife, mother of six-year-old boy twins, gave birth to another son. The twins were invited to inspect. After a long silence the mother said: 'Have yer got nowt to say to yer new brother?'

'Aye,' one child replied, 'wheerst t' other?'

Once Upon a Time

Once upon a time there was a prince and a princess and they were friends and they played games together and they had fun. Then they had a wedding and after the wedding they went home and then they had some lunch and they had a drink and then they had some pudding. Then they did some palace work.

Then they watched a bit of TV and then they had a bit of tea and a drink and then they had some pudding. Then they went to bed. The next day they had a bit of breakfast and then they had a biscuit and then they had a drink and then they had some pudding. Then they went downstairs and then they got dressed and then they went to hospital and then they had a baby. Then they went home and they had a bit of tea and then they had some pudding.

Jennifer and Claire

My grandson started school in September. After his first week, he came home to say that the teacher had told them that there were three brothers in the class with the same birthday and that they were called 'twiglets'.

—

John, aged three and born a bred on a Dales farm, went to see his mother in hospital to view his new baby brother. He was less interested in the new addition to his family but was fascinated by a black woman in the next bed with her little baby.

'Don't stare,' said John's mum to her little boy, 'it's very rude.'

The black woman smiled and waved, then got out of bed to take the baby for his feed. She put on a white dressing gown and white socks. As she was heading for the door little John, pointing at her, announced: 'Swaledale.'

That's the Head Mystery's room

School and schooldays

Teachers take on the most important role in society: the education of the young. Teaching is demanding, challenging and sometimes frustrating, but there are few jobs which are as exciting and fulfilling. Those who take on this most important role must, of course, be prepared to meet little philosophers and sharp critics, the curious, the precocious, the unpredictable, the charming and, sometimes, the exasperating.

A fellow school inspector was visiting the infant classroom and engaged a little boy in a conversation about dinosaurs.

'You know a lot about these creatures,' he said.

'I know.' The little boy looked up. 'I luv 'em. They're great. I draw 'em all t' time.'

'And are there any around today?'

'Cooarse not. They're all deead. They're hextinct.'

'What does that mean?'

'Deead. Wiped aaht.'

'And why do you think that is?' the inspector asked.

The little boy had thought for a moment. 'Well, mester,' he said, 'that's one of life's gret mysteries, in't it?'

I was once told by a little girl that her auntie had got sixty-five roses.

'Sixty-five roses?' I said. 'She's very lucky your auntie, isn't she?'

The child shook her head. 'No, she's not. It's not nice having sixty-five roses.'

'I thought your auntie would really like so many beautiful coloured flowers with their lovely smell.'

'It's not nice having sixty-five roses.' she persisted quietly.

And then it dawned upon me. Her auntie had just died. These were the flowers at her funeral.

'Has your auntie died?' I asked gently.

'No,' said the child in a voice deep with indignation. 'She's got sixty-five roses.' The teacher, hearing the exchange, and seeing my puzzlement and the child's, explained with a wry smile, 'She means cystic fibrosis, Mr Phinn.'

Teachers

Teachers shout and bawl at us
Making such a massive fuss.
Homework comes in piles and piles,
Essays last for miles and miles.
They give us sums we cannot do
And never think of something new.
Same boring lessons every week
Sending children off to sleep,
Same droning voices every day
How I wish they'd go away.

Andrew (aged nine)

'And when Chicken Licken arrived at the palace, children,' the infant teacher informed her little charges, 'and told the king that the sky was falling down, what do you think the king said?'

'Bloody hell, a talking chicken', replied an infant.

—

Jennie, my daughter, when five, came home and said she had to take something old to school.

'You can take me,' I told her.

'Oh no,' she exclaimed. 'It has to be something precious.'

—

My grandson's school was undergoing a school inspection. I asked Jordan how things were going. 'We're being infected, Grannie,' he told me, 'and I don't like it.'

On Monday Mr Dobson came
into school He was fat
with wiskers and a flat
cap. He wouldeht stop
talking. He got boring and
we fell asleep. Mrs wilson
Said he liked the sound
of his own voice.

The School Inspector Calls

On Monday Mr Dobson came into school. He was fat with whiskers and a flat cap. He wouldn't stop talking. He got boring and we fell asleep. Mrs Wilson said he liked the sound of his own voice.

Amy (aged six)

I taught in an inner-city infant school. Many of the children, although from poor and often difficult backgrounds, were warm and loving. I was reading the story of 'The Three Little Pigs', and told my little charges how the Big Bad Wolf was intent on blowing down the house of straw and gobbling up the first little pig. 'The bastard!' came a small voice from the back.

—

I help voluntarily at a junior and infant school. One of the teachers mentioned to the children that it was my seventieth birthday. A little one piped up: 'Ah, Mrs Thompson, aren't you glad that you are still alive?'

—

Our young daughter Carmel, coming home, was asked by my wife what had happened at school that day. She answered: 'Oh, we have a new headmonster.'

Visit to the Farm

Last Tuesday we went to Wilson's Farm. My friend Mark was sick on the bus – all over the seat, his shoes, his coat and Mrs Thompson. She went mad and smelt horrible. Mark had to put his head in a big blue plastic bucket. Mrs Thompson pulled faces all the way. When we got to the farm, Mark trod in some cow pats.

Mr Wilson, the farmer, said, 'Pooh! Something smells worse than my pigs.'

Mrs Thompson went bright red. Farmer Wilson showed us some horses and pigs and big cows and hens and geese. Then he pointed to a field. 'Look at those heifers,' but I couldn't see any.

Geoffrey (aged six)

Child showing round a new boy: 'That's the Head Mystery's room.'

———

Two infant children in Leeds caught sight of a squirrel outside the classroom window.

'Quick, tell Miss,' cried one.

'Shut yer gob, Gavin,' replied the other. 'She'll 'ave us write abaat the bugger.'

My School

My school is horrid. They give you rotten milk and I can tell you how rotten the milk is. In Class 1, I could not drink all my milk, 'cos it is so rotten so I decided to make a plan.

My teacher was away and the class was took over by Miss Martin and I could not drink it fast because it was so rotten and when the class went out to play, I emptied my milk into the sink and went out to play and Jimmy Bennet was surprised to see

me at play but I didn't mind 'cos God had made me very glad but now I'm in Class Two. I've got good at drinking milk but there was another problem –

Sums. So I got another plan in my head and do you know what it was? It was to cheat. I counted in ones by putting ones all the way up my book until I had sixteen. And that was what the number was at the top of my page so that was another problem dealt with but there was another problem what no one could get rid of but I could and that was writing. So I got near a boy with chicken pox so I could not go to school.

Geoffrey (aged seven)

When I was headteacher of an infant school some years ago, I was telling a small child off for some misdemeanor. He had been throwing stones at other children. He tried to extricate himself from his difficult situation without success and was clearly losing the argument. Then he played his trump card. Wiping away his tears, he took a deep breath and told me pathetically: 'And I'm from a one-parent family, you know.'

—

My grandson Richard, when he was six, wrote in his school journal; 'Last night my daddy beat my mummy again.' He was, as his mother explained to the concerned teacher, referring to Scrabble.

—

The school inspector sat with the infants at lunch. The pudding was a particularly hard and brittle piece of biscuit, and when he tried to stab it with his spoon, it jumped up and out of the bowl. 'Tha wants to put some custard on it, mester,' advised the small boy sitting opposite, 'to stop it leeapin' abaat.'

To Granny and family
Love from Sarah

Friendes

Granny   Linda   Samantha   Rory

Sofie

And the greatest of these is love

Children are powerfully affected by those around them. Well before they can speak, they are able understand so much – a smile, a gentle touch, the tone of our voice, a frown. Their great desire in life, as it is for all of us, is to be loved.

When my eldest son Richard graduated from Durham University, the chancellor, Sir Peter Ustinov, draped in his gold-trimmed academic gown and sporting a very impressive mortar board, was interrupted in his address by the loud and happy gurgling of a baby at the rear of the hall. The great man deviated from his speech, and told the young graduands that all that small innocent desired was to be fed, kept warm and to be loved and then he or she would be happy indeed. Perhaps it was a lesson for us all, he told us. The baby babbled on and the chancellor with a wonderfully serious countenance gurgled back, much to everyone's amusement. 'The child has just informed me,' he announced, 'that he is ready to be changed.'

My Sister

My little sister died last night
In the Hospital.
She was four days old.
Only four days old.
And when I saw her for the first time
I don't think I'd ever been as happy.
She was small and crinkled
With big eyes and soft, soft skin
And a smile like a rainbow.
Her fingers were like tiny sticks
And her nails were like little sea shells
And her hair like white feathers.
Now she's gone, and my mum can't stop crying,
And my dad stairs at nothing.
I loved our baby.
I'll never forget her.

James (aged ten)

My Sister.

My little sister died last night
In the Hospital.
She was four days old,
Only four days old.
And when I saw her for the first time,
I do'nt think I'd ever been as happy.
She was so small and crinkled.
With big eyes and soft soft skin.
And a smile like a rainbow.
Her fingers were like tiny sticks.
And her nails like little sea shells.
And her hair like white feathers.
Now shes gone, and my mum can't stop crying,
And my dad stairs at nothing.
I loved our baby.
I'll never forget her.

I married my lass fifty-four years ago after leaving the Scots Guards and recently lost her. I find life without her tough. One day I was feeling very down, when my grandchildren held my hands and said: 'Grandpa, we love you' — a simple expression which made an old soldier feel so much better.

—

I was shopping in Leeds with my four-year-old daughter, and in a large department store she noticed a black woman, the first she had ever seen, and was greatly interested in her. 'Mummy, Mummy, just look at that lady,' she cried, pointing. I was deeply embarrassed and dreaded a further comment. My daughter then added. 'Isn't she beautiful?' If only everybody could see the world through the eyes of a child.

—

'You know, Gran,' Amy, my six-year-old graddaughter told me when I kissed her goodnight, 'I've been thinking. If people minded their own business and loved people, there wouldn't be all this fighting in the world.'

—

'Grannie, I know what people do when they really love each other,' said Roisin, my granddaughter of six. 'I've seen it on the television.'

'Do you dear?', I said, bracing myself for a lesson in the facts of life.

Roisin nodded sagely. 'They hold each other's hands and smile.'

A Child's Prayer

Will you hug me Mummy?
Will you wrap me in your arms
And press your face to mine
And whisper happy memories in my ear.
For when shadows dance around me
And I feel alone in the dark,
I need to recall your gentle touch
And know that you are near.
Will you hold me Daddy?
Will you take my hand
And weave strong fingers into mine,
And tell me how you love me.
For when monsters invade my dreams
And I feel helpless and afraid,
I need to remember your powerful hands
And feel your strong protection.

Emily (aged sixteen)

For a full list of
Dalesman books, calendars,
videos, DVDs, cassettes
and magazines, visit
www.dalesman.co.uk
or telephone
(+44) 01756 701033

Little Angels
Gervase Phinn

Dalesman

First published in Great Britain 2006
by Dalesman Publishing
an imprint of
Country Publications Limited
The Water Mill, Broughton Hall,
Skipton, North Yorkshire BD23 3AG
www.dalesman.co.uk

Introductory text, poems and editorial selection
© Gervase Phinn 2006
Stories and illustrations
© the contributors 2006

ISBN 1 85568 236 2

Designed by Butler & Tanner Ltd
Colour origination by PPS Grasmere Limited
Printed and bound in China

PUBLISHER'S NOTE
The publisher expresses its gratitude to the children whose
stories and illustrations are reproduced in this book. Copyright is expressly
reserved on their behalf. However, given the nature of the material, it has not
been possible, despite every effort by Gervase Phinn and Country Publications
Ltd, to contact every contributor. In lieu of copyright fees,
Country Publication has made a donation to
the British Dyslexia Association.

CONTENTS

Introduction

For young children, everything around them is new, exciting and colourful, and a source of great wonder. In trying to make sense of the world, they can be charmingly entertaining and sometimes surprisingly profound.

Little Gems, the Dalesman collection of anecdotes, poems and the wise words of children published in 2004, generated a great deal of interest, and I was delighted that so many readers took the time and trouble to send me their own especial favourites. The Dalesman office was inundated with the witty remarks of children, their insightful observations on life, and their amusing and sometimes poignant comments about others – so many, in fact, that I had such a difficult task selecting the ones to publish. So we decided to compile a sequel, Little Angels, which I hope you will enjoy dipping into as much as you did with Little Gems.

For me, this book has been a labour of love, and I have laughed out loud at the letters, cards, anecdotes and memories you have so kindly sent and allowed me to share with others. I am very grateful to those who offered so much wonderful material but, sadly, space only allows me to publish no more than my own particular favourites. It has not always been possible to credit the author of every piece, for some arrived on the editor's desk without a name, so I extend my thanks to all those who contributed anonymously.

Finally, a word of thanks: to Robert Flanagan, managing director of Dalesman Publishing, for suggesting the original idea and giving me the opportunity to put together this collection; to Mark Whitley, my ever-patient editor who throughout has been good-humoured and supportive; and to my wife Christine who has helped me make the final selection – and done all the typing.

Acknowledgements

The author and publishers would like to thank the pupils and staff of the following schools for their help in providing illustrations: All Saints C of E Primary School, Aston, Sheffield; Beach Grove Elementary School, Delta, British Columbia, Canada; Cayton School, Scarborough; Christ the King RC Primary School, Thornaby, Stockton-on-Tees; Grassington CE (VC) Primary School; Leamington Primary & Nursery School, Sutton-in-Ashfield; Lydiate Primary School, Liverpool; St Andrew's School, Meads, Eastbourne; Town Field Primary School, Doncaster; Woodthorpe Community Primary School, Sheffield.

The following *Dalesman* readers have kindly contributed to the text: Judith Allott; Jean Bagshaw; Muriel Barber; D Beckett; F Beecroft; Sandra Birch; Sue Black; M C Bonser; Lilian Brooks; Barbara Buckley; Patricia Butcher; D Carter; Jean Chalk; P E Clough; Sam Cottingham; Patricia Devlin; George Evans; Janet Fairs; C Foote; Mrs B E Ford; Eileen Gibb; Andy Gilgunn; Mollie Gooch; J Gough; Alice Haddington; Letitia Halvorsen; Jeanne Hand; Yvonne Helps; Bill Horncastle; Caroline Leckenby; Tony Lilley; Mary Long; David Marshall; John Morley; Stella Morris; Peggy Radcliffe; Margaret Robson; Joan Robertshaw; Hugh Rowland; Anita Simcox; Beryl Smith; Don Smith; Norma Stephenson; A E Swindlehurst; Wyn Thompson; F M Watson; Shirley Webb; Mark Whitley; Maureen Whitley.

8

Mothers and Fathers

My parents were remarkable people. When I was young I thought that all children had fathers and mothers like mine: loving, funny, generous, ever-supportive. I thought all children had mothers who took out their false teeth and pretended to be witches, and fathers who told wild and wonderful stories, recited monologues ('Albert and the Lion', 'Brown Boots', 'The Green Eye of the Little Yellow God'), and pretended to be monsters and chase them round the living room, growling and grunting.

I thought all children were surrounded with books – fairy tales and fables, nursery rhymes and riddles, Peter Rabbit, the Famous Five, Biggles – and had their own little library of favourites – *Treasure Island, Moonfleet, White Fang, Kidnapped, The Thirty-Nine Steps, King Solomon's Mines* – and, through reading, inhabited a far-off world of excitement and adventure.

I imagined that all homes had books and stories, music and laughter, courtesy and good manners, honesty and love. It is only now I am older, and have met countless numbers of children in the schools I have visited, that I appreciate just how special my parents were and how hard they tried to bring the four of us up to be honest and decent young people. Now, in later life, I know for sure that the relationship between a child and his or her parents is the most critical influence on that child's life.

When I was a Boy

When I was a boy:
My bunk bed was a pirate ship
That sailed the seven seas,
My sheets they were the silvery sails
That fluttered in the breeze.

I'd dream of clashing cutlasses
And the crack, crack, crack of the gun
And the boom, boom, boom of the cannons
And the heat of the tropical sun.

I'd dream of far-off oceans
And treasure by the ton,
And mountainous waves
And watery graves
And islands in the sun.

My young daughter arrived home with two little friends from down the street.

'Have you come to see the new baby?' I asked.

'No,' said my daughter, 'I told Amy and Hannah they could watch you when you breast feed. They wouldn't believe me when I told them about it.' —

My little six-year-old son placed his tooth under the pillow for the Tooth Fairy. Since my eyesight is not what it was and his bedroom was dark, I exchanged the tooth for what I thought was a £1 coin. Next morning he came down to breakfast very peeved, holding a one-euro piece, and commented, 'French tooth fairies don't give you as much as the English ones.'

———

Eight-year-old daughter, pointing a little finger at her father before he took her with two friends to Brownies: 'Daddy, before we set off, can we get something straight – no singing in front of my friends.'

———

My young daughter, aged seven, told her younger sister that it was good in the juniors because all the children had 'chicken coops'. Intrigued, I asked her to describe this 'chicken coop'.

'It's where you put your books and things,' she explained. 'It's called a chicken coop.'

She meant 'pigeon hole'.

———

My son, a little Yorkshire tyke, aged ten, lost a tooth and that night placed it under his pillow.

'I can't believe that you still believe in the Tooth Fairy,' I told him.

'I'd believe owt,' he replied, 'if there's money in it.'

———

We were taking our nine-year-old son to the cinema one Saturday evening and caught the bus into town. On the seat opposite us was a youth obviously out clubbing and wearing a garish T-shirt emblazoned with the words 'Oh God, please let me score tonight!'

'What team do you play for?' asked my son innocently.

—

On a flight to Florida my son, aged six, was very excited. He had never been on an aeroplane before and was eager for it to take off. The woman in the next seat was clearly not as keen and closed her eyes as the plane taxied down the runway, engines roaring. My son turned to her and said: 'Let's hope it doesn't crash'.

—

After a display by the dolphins at a zoo, the keeper asked if there was anything the children might like to ask. My young son's question fairly stumped him: 'Don't you think that the dolphins would be happier swimming in the sea instead of doing tricks?'

—

At the pantomime the Ugly Sisters, played by two large and very deep-voiced men, invited children, including my son, onto the stage to ask them questions. When Griselda, one of the sisters, asked him if there was anything he wanted to ask, he looked up and enquired: 'Are you two gay then?'

—

Good
Work

Whilst preparing lengths of wood to be used as flooring in the loft and ably assisted by my four-year-old daughter, she noticed a pile of sawdust where the sawing had taken place.

'Look, daddy,' she cried. 'Crumbs.'

—

My daughter used to spend a long time playing in the bath when she was young. One day, when she eventually got out, her toes were red and wrinkled. She looked at them thoughtfully before announcing. 'I'm all shrinkled.'

—

Son Ian, aged eight, was chattering away fifty to the dozen. I told him to slow down as I couldn't understand what he was saying, adding that he was talking far too quickly.

'I am not talking too quickly,' he told me. 'It's you who are listening too slowly.'

—

I was playing tennis with my seven-year-old daughter when she stopped me in my tracks with the following observation: 'You know, mum, if it wasn't for your face, you'd look about nineteen.'

—

'One day, mummy,' said Lauren, 'I want to get married.'

'Well, he'll be a very lucky boy,' I replied.

'I'm not getting married yet,' she said, horrified. 'You have to be really old and if you pick the wrong person you're stuck with him for the rest of your life.'

'You mean like me and daddy?' I asked jokingly.

'Exactly,' she replied, seriously.

—

My daughter, Lizzie, then aged five: 'Quick mummy, come and look out of the window.'

I looked out to see two dogs mating in the middle of the street.

'Aren't they clever,' says Lizzie. 'They've learnt to do circus tricks.'

———

I was in a family hotel on the Fylde coast, when it was bed-time for one little boy. As his dad approached to carry him off to their room, up the child jumped on his chair, pointed at his father and shouted at the top of his voice: 'Knob head! Knob head! Knob head!' As his embarrassed father swept up the child in his arms and walked past me to the lift, he saw my shocked expression and leaned across to explain.

'It's not what you think,' he said. 'What he was saying was "No bed! No bed! No bed!"'

———

One day I told my small son that the next day, Friday, was pay-day, to which he replied, 'Dad, if you only get paid on Friday, why do you work all those other days.'

———

One year I brought my son, Michael, aged ten, over to the UK on holiday. One day we had bought our tickets and were running for a train. A porter said to us, 'Rushing, are you?'

Michael, with an amazed look on his face said, 'No, we're from Canada.'

———

22

My son, Adam, aged six, gave me a Father's Day card he had done at school. The teacher had asked the children to write an acrostic where the letter at the beginning of each line, when read downwards, spells the father's name. He wrote:

Watches telly,

Is a supporter of Sheffield Wednesday,

Likes a drink,

Likes to stay in bed,

Is quite fat,

Always spends a long time in the bath,

Makes me smile.

—

My son, aged seven, just would not go to sleep and was told that if he got out of bed again he would be in serious trouble.

'Can I have a drink of water?' he shouted from his bedroom.

'Go to sleep!'

'But can I have a drink of water?'

'No!'

'But I'm thirsty.'

'You should have had a drink before you got into bed.'

'But I'm thirsty.'

'Go to sleep!'

'Pleeeeaaaase.'

'If I come up those stairs, young man, it will be to smack your bottom.'

'Well, when you come up to smack my bottom, will you bring me a glass of water?'

—

I was a month from my thirty-ninth birthday when my youngest son was born. He attended the village school until the age of nine, when he transferred to the middle school in the next village. One day after a week or two he came home highly excited: 'Mum, mum, I have found someone whose mum is older than you!'

———

'My daddy has false teeth,' said my little daughter. 'They come out in a group.'

———

We were on our way back after a day out in Whitby one Sunday and pulled into a market garden outside Pickering.

'What does it mean,' asked my six-year-old, 'if you roger somebody?'

I was taken aback. 'Where did you hear that word?' I asked.

He pointed to the sign in the car park: 'Welcome to Roger Market Garden.'

———

My daughter, Rachel, a bridesmaid at her sister's wedding, was all ears when the vicar asked the bride, 'Do you take this man for better or worse, for richer or poorer, in sickness and in health?'

'Say richer,' whispered Rachel.

———

My son, when we were out for a walk on a very bright, sparkly, frosty morning: 'Look Mummy, the grass has got its lights on.'

———

On our way out for a picnic a few years ago we were passing two reservoirs. I pointed these out to our daughter and told her these were where we got our water.

'Which is the hot one, then?' came the quick reply.

———

24

My daughter tucked up Kara for the night and was leaving the bedroom when Kara said, 'Put the dark on, Mummy.'

—

Many years ago when our children, Steven and Julia, were about seven and five years of age, we used to take them out most Sundays visiting sights and museums. Afterwards we always had a little quiz on what they had seen.

One Sunday we took the Tube into London, visiting various places including the City, Threadneedle Street and the Stock Exchange. Later we were sitting on the Embankment having an ice cream, when we had the quiz.

I asked, 'What do we call the Old Lady of Threadneedle Street?'

'Maggie Thatcher,' replied Steven.

26

Grannies and Grandpas

Grannies and grandpas have a very special relationship with their grandchildren. It is self-evident that they have more experience with children, greater understanding and infinitely more patience. They love to see their grand-children but are thankful that they can give them back at the end of the day.

Our family was by no means well off, but my Grandma Mullarkey managed the small amount of money meticulously. She would shop judiciously and was always on the look-out for a bargain. Once, my mother told me, she recalled visiting the fish counter at Sheffield Castle Market. Grandma, looking elegant in her Sunday best, asked for any fish heads, which she would use to make the most delicious soup. 'For the cat,' she told the fishmonger.

'We haven't got a cat,' my mother piped up with all the honesty of the young child.

'Yes we have,' said grandma, giving her a knowing look and a wink.

'No we haven't,' persisted my mother, to all in earshot. 'My mum boils up the fish heads in a big pot over the fire for our tea.'

Letter to Grannie and Grampa

Dear Grannie and Grampa,
Mother's come out in a rash,
Father's got the mumps,
Richard's got a tummy ache,
Dominic's got lumps.
Mum's got German measles,
But there's nothing wrong with me,
And I cannot wait for Sunday,
When you're coming round for tea.

Interrogation in the Nursery

Infant: What's that on your face?
Inspector: It's a moustache.
Infant: Can I have one?
Inspector: No, little girls don't have moustaches.
Infant: Can I have one when I grow up?
Inspector: No, ladies don't have moustaches either.
Infant: Well, my grannie's got one.

I was reading a pop-up picture book about animals with my young granddaughter, aged three, which made an animal noise appropriate to the creature on the page. With each sound I asked her to guess what creature she thought it might be. The tiger snarled, the bison grunted and the monkey chattered. I paused to blow my nose. 'Elephant,' she cried.

—

I was looking in the mirror and observed, speaking to my nine-year-old granddaughter, that I had lots of wrinkles and that I perhaps needed a facelift.

'No, granny,' she exclaimed. 'Don't go to one of the drastic surgeons.'

—

When I asked my young grandson what Father Christmas was bringing him for Christmas, he shouted, 'A BIKE! I'M GETTING A BIKE!'

'You have no need to shout,' I told him, 'Father Christmas is not deaf, you know.'

'I know,' he replied, 'but daddy's upstairs and he might not hear me.'

—

While shopping with my granddaughter, aged four, we went into a café for a cup of tea and a sandwich. When the beautifully garnished sandwiches arrived, my granddaughter announced in a very loud voice: 'I am not eating them! They are full of weeds.'

—

Little Robert, my grandson, aged four, was looking curiously at trays of bedding plants waiting to be planted in the garden. The trays, with the exception of one, were clearly labelled.

'Grandma, what are those flowers called?' he asked.

'Oh dear, Robert,' I said as I touched my brow, 'I can't remember. It's at the back of my mind.'

'Well, grandma,' he suggested, 'just tip your head forward and it might come out.'

—

My granddaughters Georgina and Jessica, aged four, asked if they could go outside to play. 'You go out first, granddad,' said Georgina. 'You'll be able to tell if it's raining because you're bald.'

—

In a doctor's surgery my grandson approached an elderly man in a wheelchair and asked him, 'Can you do wheelies in that?'

—

Recently my grandson's teacher was complimenting him on his work and asked, 'Who do you take after?'

My grandson replied, 'That's easy. I take after my grandfather – he used to be intelligent.'

—

The time had arrived when I had to say goodbye to my son and his family, and return to my home in Australia, after spending a wonderful holiday with them. It was a very emotional time so I decided to make my departures when they were busily eating lunch. I was determined to leave without them knowing that my heart was near to breaking.

'Well,' I said, in a trembling voice, 'I've sewn all the name tags on your school clothes, I've tidied your rooms, I've made lunch and now it's time for me to say goodbye. Is there anything you want to say before I go?'

'Could you pass the tomato sauce please?' asked Edward, aged six.

—

On grandma's seventieth birthday, all the family gathered around the table for a celebration meal. The highlight was when William, aged ten, brought in the beautifully iced and

33

grandma

grandad

34

decorated birthday cake. Grandma, duly touched, asked, looking towards her daughter with love and gratitude, 'And who did all the hard work with the cake?'

'Marks and Spencer,' replied William.

———

Jamie's great-grandfather was in the Second World War and distinguished himself fighting in the Western Desert. When he came out of the army he joined the fire service, and there too took on a dangerous and difficult job of work. On several occasions he risked his own life. When he retired he had a triple heart bypass and survived prostate cancer.

At a children's playground, Jamie asked his great-grandfather if he would like to go down the slide and, when he received the reply that it was not for him, Jamie shook his head, looked at his great-grandfather pityingly, and said, 'Come on great-gramps, don't be such a wimp.'

———

A few years ago the family were at my mother's for her birthday, when out of the blue my young nephew, who had been learning about evolution at school, asked: 'Nanna, did you use to be a monkey?'

———

I have fine surface veins on the back of my legs and when I took my three-year-old grandson swimming his comments were, 'Who has been drawing maps on the back of your legs, grandma?'

———

Joshua, aged seven: 'Grandma, your hands feel like pizza dough.'

———

Jake was around two years old and loved to play hide-and-seek, his favourite hiding place being behind the long curtains. It was just before Christmas and he had been taken by his grandmother to the children's Christingle service at her local church. The service was about to start and the vicar hurried down the aisle and disappeared into the vestry, behind a curtain. This did not go unnoticed by Jake, and he was out of his seat in a flash and racing down the aisle.

'Come on, nanna,' he shouted. 'Hiding.'

—

As I was reading the story of *Peter Pan* to my granddaughter Emma, aged four, she asked: 'Granddad, what did they call Captain Hook before he lost his arm?'

—

My grandson and I were playing with his Lego on the carpet, and I had my head down over the piece I was building. 'Granddad,' my grandson said, 'do you know that the top of your head is growing through your hair?'

—

Foolishly I was persuaded by my grandson to go down the water chute at a leisure centre. Being 'amply proportioned', I got stuck halfway down. It was only with the help of the teenager sliding down behind me, who crashed into me and dislodged me, that I managed to make it to the bottom. I was catapulted into the water with the very embarrassed young man on top of me. Surfacing, I found the attendant blowing his whistle shrilly and ordering me out. My grandson, who had been watching proceedings, said as I staggered towards him, wet, bedraggled and shame-faced, 'Can you do that again, grannie?'

—

My grandsons Alister and Fraser, aged six and seven, were playing soldiers at war. I told them I had lived through World War Two when a little girl, explaining why I had to wear gas masks and ear plugs, and also having to go into air-raid shelters when German planes came over to drop bombs. They both stood looking at me in awe, then Fraser asked, 'But grandma, why aren't you dead?'

—

I was singing in the bathroom when my grandson's head appeared about the door. He is seven and has just started at a rather posh preparatory school.

'Grandpa,' he said, 'cut out the singin', you're doin' mi 'ead in.'

—

My young grandson was suffering from a bout of low self-esteem. His dad was doing his best to convince him that he was indeed a bright, clever and popular young man, but wasn't getting through. Eventually his dad asked: 'Have I ever lied to you?'

'Well,' Jonathan replied, 'you did about Father Christmas.'

—

My great-niece wanted to know how old I was.

'I don't know,' I said mischievously.

'You ought to know how old you are,' she said. 'I know how old I am.'

'Well,' I said, 'I must have forgotten.'

'Well, look in your knickers, granny,' she said.

'Look in my knickers,' I repeated intrigued, 'and how will that help?'

'It tells you how old you are on the label. Mine says for a 5–7 year old.'

—

40

I was dancing to 'Chirpy, Chirpy, Cheep, Cheep' at the reception after my grandson's wedding and as I left the floor, I was taken aside by my very serious great-grandson. 'Granny,' he said, 'a bit of advice. You're too old for that sort of thing.'

———

My son had been looking at some old black-and-white family photographs. When he next saw his granddad he asked, 'Were you alive, granddad, when the world was black and white?'

———

This exchange took place recently between my three-year-old grandson Adam and me when looking in a drawer in our house for a favourite toy:

'Oh dear, Adam, this drawer is in an awful muddle – I expect the toys in your room are all nice and tidy.'

Adam, in all seriousness, 'Oh no, granny, our house is a mess – just like yours.'

———

My young granddaughter, Amy, was in the back of my car one day when I, forgetting for a moment that she was with me, referred to the driver in front of me as 'a prat'.

Amy then asked, 'And is the lady with him Mrs Prat?'

———

A few gems from the grandchildren:

'Mummy puts rhododendron under her arms.'

'Oh dear, every time granddad gets a good idea it makes life difficult.'

'We've been to the theatre to see the Sugar Lump Fairy.'

'Aunty Di hasn't any children of her own so she has to use me.'

'Aren't I lucky to have a nan and granddad who aren't dead.'

———

My friend's granddaughter was looking at her intently, then said, 'You should use some of that wrinkle cream advertised on the telly. I'll bring you some,' which she did the next time she called. A few days later her grandma came under close scrutiny again.

'Are you still using that cream, grandma?'

'Yes,' she answered.

'Doesn't work very well, does it?' came the honest reply.

—

On the telephone with my granddaughter, aged four and a half.

Lauren: Happy birthday, Pappa.

Pappa: Thank you, Lauren.

Lauren: How old are you today?

Pappa: I'm sixty-nine. I expect that seems very old to you.

Lauren (without hesitation): That's not very old, Pappa – it's just really grown-up.

—

My granddaughter Jenny, aged six, painted a colourful picture and brought it to show me.

'Why, that's lovely, Jenny. What is it?' I said.

She gave me a scathing and rather pitying look, and replied 'A *real* artist doesn't have to say what it is, Grandma.'

—

My grandson had just started school and was very fond of his diary. One entry was: 'My grandma has cat biscuits and shoe polish for breakfast.' He was referring to the latest breakfast cereals and my Marmite on toast.

—

A few years ago my wife and I, accompanied by our four-year-old grandson, were walking into the town centre by way of the parish church. The path through the churchyard is somewhat restricted and, to maximise the available space, old gravestones have been laid flat alongside the single-slab paving stones.

Understandably our grandson was about to walk on the gravestones when we stopped him, saying they belonged to people who had died and were buried in the churchyard.

'What are gravestones?' he asked. We replied they were in remembrance of those people, and written on the stones were their names, ages and often kind messages and verses were included in honour of the deceased.

'Oh, like get-well-soon cards?' our grandson rejoined.

–

Giving my granddaughter, aged three, a piggyback home, she said: 'Granddad, when are you going to get a *proper* job – not this teaching thing?' I was headteacher of a comprehensive school at the time.

44

Uncles and Aunts

My Auntie Nora and my mother trained as nurses. Nora was quite a beauty and had a succession of eligible beaus. At the time when she was sister-in-charge of the casualty department at Doncaster Royal Infirmary she was 'walking out' with a doctor, much to the delight of my grandmother, who had very high hopes for her children.

Auntie Nora was a great storyteller. She would tell tales about when she was training to be a nurse. Mischievous doctors would send her up to ward nine for a couple of Fallopian tubes. Once, the surgeon in the operating theatre asked her to fetch sister's coat. Thinking it was another ruse, my aunt refused. The surgeon exploded and demanded that she fetch sister's coat as instructed. 'Do as you are told, nurse!' ordered the theatre sister, as red-faced and furious as the surgeon. My aunt scurried off and returned with sister's coat. The surgeon bit his lip, looked heavenwards and, controlling his temper, informed my aunt it was the cystoscope which he required.

Uncle Alex was dad's elder brother. He was a highly decorated officer in the Royal Air Force and flew as a navigator during the War. I have his eight medals, which include the MBE, on my wall. Uncle Alex looked and spoke like a character out of my *Biggles* books. He was tall and lithe, with a great ginger handlebar moustache and hands like spades. He would appear at the door, with his brown canvas bag, stay for a few days and then depart. Once he arrived in the early morning and climbed though a window to gain entry. He then settled down on the settee in the front room only to be confronted later by my father brandishing a poker and assuming he had burglars.

It was Uncle Alec who attempted to show me how to play cricket.

Unlucky Uncle Alec

Unlucky Uncle Alec
While one day playing cricket,
Saw a four-leaf clover
And thought that he would pick it.
As he bent down towards the ground,
To pluck the lucky leaf,
The cricket ball flew through the air
And knocked out all his teeth.
He shouted 'Drat!' and dropped the bat,
Which landed on his toes,
It bounced back up and cracked his chin,
Then smacked him on the nose.
Smeared in blood and caked in mud,
He said, 'I'm glad that's over,'
Then with a sigh, he held up high,
His lucky four-leaf clover.

When my young niece, Jade, aged six, was visiting, she was very taken with my new outfit.

'You look really nice, Auntie Christine,' she said sweetly.

'Thank you, Jade,' I said, 'that's very nice of you to say.'

'And I really really like your dress.'

'Do you?'

'Mummy's got some curtains like it.'

—

49

Having spent yet another weekend with his two old aunties in the country while his parents were away, Little Sam was asked to say thank you.

'Go on, Sam, say "thank you for having me"', urged his mother.

Sam reluctantly obliged. Aunty Dora patted his little head and said, 'You'll come and see us again, won't you?', to which Sam replied, 'Only if I'm forced!'

—

'You might not be as tall as daddy,' said my young son to his Uncle Michael, 'but you're a lot, lot wider.'

—

Aunty was watching the funeral service of Sir Winston Churchill on the television with her little nephew. As the coffin was carried into the church he suddenly said: 'I know what they are going to do now. They're going to open the box.'

—

My young nephew, all of eight, came to visit. His father is a barrister, his mother a solicitor. I had lost my glasses, and searched high and low without success.

'Now, let's think about this logically,' he said seriously. 'Can you recall where you last had them?'

He clearly was to follow in his parents' footsteps.

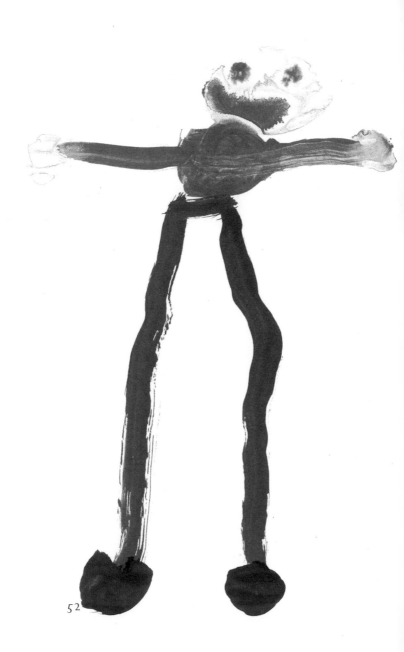

52

Friends and Neighbours

When I was growing up in Rotherham, Mr Evans, our next-door neighbour, was incredibly bow-legged and waddled down his garden path, much to our amusement. Dad told me the reason for Mr Evans' unusual gait. Before I was born, Mrs Evans had been painting the bathroom windowsills. She cleaned her brush in turpentine substitute and then poured the remains of the very inflammable liquid down the toilet. Mr Evans, so dad related, was wont to sit on the toilet reading his paper and enjoying his pipe. You might predict the outcome that particular morning. Mrs Evans had not flushed the toilet so, when her poor unsuspecting husband tapped the smouldering remains of his pipe down between his legs and into the toilet bowl, there was a great flash followed by terrible screams. The ambulance duly arrived but, when a distraught Mrs Evans explained how the unfortunate casualty had suffered such severe burns to his nether regions, the ambulance men, halfway down the stairs, became convulsed with laughter and dropped the stretcher, causing Mr Evans to tumble out and break both legs. Hence, dad explained, the poor man's unusual way of walking.

Our other neighbour Mrs Rogers frequently popped in for a cup of tea and a chat with mum, and I – a little boy of six or seven – would sit playing with my Lego or train set, listening. Sometimes the conversation would be *sotto voce* when the topic was not for 'little ears' and I had to strain to listen. 'He's a wolf in sheep's clothing, that one,' Mrs Rogers would say or 'She's no better than she should be – all fur coat and no knickers'. I've always had a great deal to say, but I have also been a keen listener and a sharp observer of people. I suppose writers have to be magpies, collecting gobbets of conversation, little gems of language, quirks of character, accents and mannerisms, because that is from where they get the material for their stories and poems.

When my neighbour's garden fence blew down in the wind, crushing my flowers and smashing all the glass in my cold frame, I was angry and upset. Our grandson Tom, all of six years old, put his hands on his hips and shook his little head before saying, 'You know what I always say, granddad, it's not the end of the world.'

—

When a friend of mine died, I told my small grandson how much I would miss her and how I wished she were still alive. He watched me as I wrote a black-edged 'In Memoriam' card, adding 'RIP' after her name.

'What does 'RIP' mean, grannie?' he asked.

'Each letter stands for a word,' I told him.

'Return if possible?' he asked.

—

'What's a coot?' my little boy asked our neighbour, who was mowing the lawn at the front of his house.

'It's a bird, I think,' said Mr Martin. 'Why do you want to know?'

'My dad says you're like a coot.'

'Are you sure he said coot?' asked our neighbour, intrigued.

'Well, he said you were as bald as one.'

—

Mr Evans, our next-door neighbour, was feeling rather down when his dog, Jessie, died. My son, aged six, trying to cheer him up, used a favourite expression of his grandpa's ('Keep your pecker up') but didn't quite get it right. He told a rather surprised Mr Evans to 'Keep your plonker up'.

—

A friend of mine works in the local library in the children's section. Young people frequently come in asking for a book but they are not certain of the title. She's been asked for Harry Potter's 'Gobbit of Fire' and a version of 'Willy Wonker and the Chocolate Factory' (I will leave it to your imagination as to what the child asked for).

A very popular series used to be 'Nancy Drew and the Hardy Boys'. One child asked her, 'Have you any books about "Hardy Drew and the Nancy Boys"?'

Another popular series with young girls was the 'Sweet Dreams Series'. One innocent asked my friend if there were any books in the 'Wet Dreams Series'.

—

Little Kevin kept asking his mum to take him to the toilet. Mum was talking to her friends so didn't hear him. I said I would take him and Kevin asked, 'OK, but can you wipe bums?'

—

My next door neighbour's little girl, Juliet, aged eight, came home after visiting her new baby brother in hospital. She told me: 'He won't be home yet because he's very small and has to be kept in an incinerator.'

—

I am seventy-seven, and was mowing my lawn at the front of the house when the little boy whose parents had just moved in next door asked me, 'Have you a bike?'

'I have,' I replied.

'So do you want to come out to play then?'

I felt seventy years younger.

—

59

I once had a spell as a door-to-door salesman. In my first inexperienced days I called at one house where a small boy opened the door to my knock.

'Is there no one else in?' I asked.

'Yes, my sister,' said the boy brightly.

'Perhaps I could see her,' I said.

He disappeared and did not return for several minutes. Then I heard a voice calling,

'You'd better come in, mister, I can't lift her out of the playpen myself.'

Teachers and Preachers

I am five. The photograph shows a chubby little boy with a round, pale face, a mop of black hair and large eyes, sitting on the back step of the house in Richard Road, taken just before he sets off for his first day at school. I am wearing a crisp white shirt and little tartan clip-on tie, short trousers which I eventually grow into, socks pulled up to the dimpled knees and large polished black shoes. I do not look at all happy. In fact, I seem on the verge of tears.

Broom Valley Infant School appeared to a small boy of five as a vast, cold and frightening castle of a building with its huge square metal-framed windows and endless echoey corridors, shiny green tiles, hard wooden floors, and the oppressive smell of stale cabbage and floor polish. It was a daunting place and on my first day, so my mother told me years later when my own children started school, I screamed and shouted, tugged and writhed as she held my small hand firmly in hers on our way to the entrance. I hated it, and wanted to go home and sit at the table in the kitchen, and help my mother make gingerbread men and listen to her stories. When I saw her head for the door I thought I would be abandoned forever and couldn't be consoled. 'I want to go home!' I cried. 'I want to go home!' But I was made to stay and I spent the whole morning whimpering in a corner, resisting the kind attentions of Miss Greenhalgh, the infant teacher. At morning playtime I couldn't be coaxed to eat the biscuit or drink the milk on offer and continued to sniffle and whimper.

But by lunchtime I had become intrigued and soon dried my tears. Just before lunch, Miss Greenhalgh opened a large coloured picture book and began to read. I loved books, and the bedtime routine was my mother or father or sister snuggling up with me to read. I knew all the nursery rhymes and the fairy stories and, although I couldn't read, I knew if a word was changed or a bit missed out and would tell the reader so. When Miss Greenhalgh opened the book on that first morning, I stopped the sniffling and listened. She looked to me like someone out of the pages of a fairy tale: long golden hair like Rapunzel's, large blue eyes like Snow White's, and such a gentle voice and lovely smile like Sleeping Beauty's. When she started reading the story, I was completely captivated. The following morning I wolfed down my breakfast, keen to get back to school and Miss Greenhalgh.

65

Tantrum!

'I'll stamp my feet!
I'll make a fuss!
I'll squeal and screech and shout!
I'll kick my legs!
I'll bang my head!
I'll wave my hands about!
I'll bring the roof down with the noise!
I'll shriek and scream and howl!
I'll cry and yell and bellow and bawl!
I'll wail and whoop and yowl!
I just won't go to school today,
With all the girls and boys,
I want to stay at home instead,
And play with all my toys.'

'Now come along,' his mother said,
'And do not act the fool.
Get out of bed, you sleepy head
You're headteacher of the school!'

The vicar caught a boy smoking.
    'Do you know where little boys who smoke go to?' he asked .
    'Aye,' replied the boy, 'up top o' t' ginnel.'

—

Our lady curate, who usually goes into the local primary school in her normal clothes except for her collar, had brought the class of eight-year-olds into church to demonstrate a baptism complete with mum and baby. For this occasion she had put on her cassock and she asked the children if they could see anything different about her. The first little boy put up his hand and said, 'Yes, you are wearing your God suit.'

—

A vicar, with the word 'grace' in mind, asked the children, 'Does anyone know what is said before you eat?'

'I know what my dad says,' said a child. '"Go easy on the butter".'

—

The parish priest was visiting and, before leaving, asked in a rather hushed voice if he could use the toilet. As he headed for the door my little daughter, Anna, aged six, shouted after him: 'And don't forget to put the seat down and flush the toilet when you've finished.'

—

When my sister was about four we had a surprise visit from our new priest. My mum went to make a cup of tea for him and made sure that the bathroom was tidy with a clean towel. My sister used the loo later and, running into the lounge, she said in a big voice, 'Mum, who owns the new towel in the bathroom?'

—

All the same all the same in Sunshine and the rain No matter How You are you now you love so all the same

69

Dominic was all ready to go to church for his first Holy Communion, dressed in pristine white shirt, black bow tie, carefully pressed shorts, grey socks and polished black shoes.

'You look lovely, darling,' cooed granny, 'quite the little angel in your smart new outfit.'

'Yes,' he replied scowling, 'and my dad says it was a real bugger to iron.'

—

I took my class of seven-year-olds to the local Roman Catholic church in preparation for their first Holy Communion. The priest explained about the responses to his prayers during mass and hoped that the children would speak them loudly and clearly – particularly the final response, 'Thanks be to God'. At the mass one small boy, with a particularly loud and resonant voice, heard the priest tell the congregation to 'Go in peace, to love and serve the Lord', and he sat up smartly and responded with 'Thank Christ for that!'

—

'In the Bible,' said the Methodist minister, talking to a group of children in assembly, 'there is a very famous sentence, "He who lives by the sword will …" Can anyone complete it for me?'

One bright spark piped up, 'Will get shot by him who has a gun.'

—

The rural dean visited our school and told them he was really a sort of vicar.

'Can anyone tell me anything about vicars?' he asked.

'It rhymes with knickers,' said a child.

—

The priest processed down the aisle at mass in his embroidered cope.

'I like the dress,' said my young granddaughter.

—

A little boy arrived at our playgroup in Snaith, having recently moved with his family. His father had started work at the large Drax power station and he decided to take his young son to show him how it worked, As they approached the great cooling towers the child said: ' Ooooh, look daddy, a cloud factory.'

—

'Mummy,' said Bethany as she observed me just before I was to give birth to her brother. 'You're getting really fat.'

'I know, darling,' I replied, patting my stomach. 'That's because I have a baby in my tummy.'

She had a good look at my behind. 'Well, what have you got in your bottom?'

—

The teacher read the story of 'Little Red Riding Hood' and then asked the children to write the story in their own words. My six-year-old wrote that, 'Little Red Riding Hood had bright red tits.' She explained to the surprised teacher that she meant 'tights'.

—

Two infants talking in the school canteen over lunch.

'What have you got in your lunch box?'

'Crisps and egg sandwiches. What have you got?'

'Meat sandwiches and a yoghurt.'

'What's yoghurt?'

'It's like strawberry-flavoured snot.'

—

74

The headteacher was telling the children in assembly that Jesus said 'Love thy neighbour' and that violence was wrong. He spoke at length about the importance of being kind and considerate to each other. When the children arrived back at my classroom two little boys got in a fight.

'What did the headteacher just say about being kind and considerate to each other and violence being wrong?' I demanded as I pulled them apart.

Before they could respond, Britney, an angelic-looking girl, came forward and said, 'Give them a really good smack, miss! That'll stop them.'

—

The English language is a tricky business. The teacher explained to the infants that the two letters 'c' and 'h' when put together make the sound 'ch' as in 'chain', 'chair', 'chop' and 'champion.' She asked the children to suggest words with the initial sound 'ch'.

'Choolip,' announced a child.

—

The teacher asked the children to tell her something that had happened during their summer holidays which was interesting.

'When we were on the ferry to France,' volunteered one small girl sweetly, 'my granddad threw up into the wind.'

—

A six-year-old pupil in our school is well known for not being quite together when it comes to pens and ink. He is possibly a little on the clumsy side but seems to have learnt to live with it. One day his teacher, Mr Hook, was trying to fit a new cartridge into an ink pen belonging to another pupil who had been having difficulty. The teacher pushed the cartridge into the pen, and ink squirted out all over his desk and hands. Our six-year-old friend had been watching and smiled at the teacher, saying, 'Welcome to my world, Mr Hook.'

—

A teacher was giving the children a talk on hygiene and asked what the children did before they went to bed at night. She was expecting the predictable answers: 'wash', 'bath', 'clean your teeth', etc. One little boy raised his hand.

'Please, miss,' he announced. 'My dad pees in the sink.'

—

When I went to school I had never heard of PE – it was always gym. My son, Andrew, started school in 1964 and one day I asked him what he had been doing. Imagine my shock when he said, 'Peeing in the playground.' I was greatly relieved when I found out they had been doing their exercises outside.

—

Returning home from school, my daughter, Heather, aged seven, asked me if Jesus really was a Jew. When I told her he was, she looked puzzled.

'I always thought he was a Methodist, like us,' she said.

—

After singing 'Daisy, Daisy,' I asked my class, 'Does anyone know what they call a bicycle made for two?' I was expecting the answer 'tandem', but one boy, aged seven, answered, 'Is it a condom, miss?'

—

77

During the visit of the school inspector, who sat at the back of the infant classroom watching proceedings, the child sitting next to him continued to make rather loud and flatulent noises, with the accompanying smells. Finally the school inspector had had enough and asked the child to desist.

'For your information,' said the child boldly, 'I've got irritable bowel syndrome.'

—

'And what do you think a homeopath does?' the teacher asked my eleven-year-old son. 'Does he kill gay people?' came the reply.

—

A teacher was explaining about figurative language to the children, that winter is sometimes referred to as a person – 'Winter with his cold white hands and icy breath'. Thinking of spring, she asked, 'And what comes in like a lion and goes out like a lamb?'

'My dad,' replied a small boy.

—

'Can you move me from this table, miss?' asked an infant in my class, 'John's a bad effluence on me.'

—

Two little boys had got into a playground scrap.

'How did it start?' asked the headteacher.

'It started when John kicked me back.'

—

I was interviewing a prospective pupil, whose parents had applied to send their daughter to our preparatory school. In front of my desk sat the nervous mother and her eight-year-old daughter, who didn't look at all worried by the ordeal.

'And what do you like doing?' I asked.

'I like music,' replied the child, 'and I play the piano.'

'She's got grade four piano,' added her mother proudly.

'And I like reading.'

'She reads a book a week,' said the mother.

'And swimming,' said the child.

'She has medals,' added the mother.

'And,' – the girl looked at her mother – 'what sort of programmes do I like to watch on the television?'

—

Infant commenting on Prince Charming touring his realm with the crystal slipper in search of the love of his life: 'Well, I wouldn't try on Cinderella's slipper. I might get a verruca.'

—

'How old are you, Miss?' asked a seven-year-old. I replied that I was twenty-one. 'I bet my grandma would like her birthday to go backwards like yours,' he replied.

—

The children had been across to the parish church for their 'Wednesday in Lent' service. The vicar had been talking about caring for one another, being kind, helpful, considerate and being friendly together – no fighting, no squabbling, all living together as a happy family.

Miss Richardson, the infants' teacher, was bringing up the tail end of the crocodile and on arrival in the classroom was

met with the sight of two seven-year-old boys rolling about the floor and knocking the daylights out of each other. She hauled them up by their coat collars and demanded, 'What do you mean by behaviour like this? You've just been to church and the vicar has been talking about being kind and helpful and friendly, and I come into the room and find you carrying on in this dreadful manner. What have you got to say for yourselves?'

She was reading the riot act in no uncertain manner when another seven-year-old, not a particular angel himself, sidled up to her and said in awed tones, 'Eeeh, Mrs Richardson, won't God be mad!'

—

Lucy, aged six, had drawn a picture of Mary, Joseph, baby Jesus and the donkey on their way from Bethlehem. On the back of the donkey was a huge hairy creature with a grinning face.

'What's that?' asked the teacher.

'The flea,' replied Lucy.

The child had added a completely new meaning to the phrase, 'Take your wife and flee to Egypt.'

—

I was showing the children some pictures of the Nativity scene painted by famous artists.

'It must have been a bit crowded in the stable, miss, what with all them painters,' observed one child.

—

Just before Easter I was on playground duty and, knowing the mother of a nine-year-old girl was in hospital, I enquired how she was. 'She's fine,' she replied. 'She's coming home on Friday. She only went in for an Easter egg tummy.' (hysterectomy)

—

When I was teaching, six-year-old Alex was late for school one morning. I asked him why he was late. He replied, 'Mum's car broke down and she had to call the IRA to fix it.'

Questions and Answers

In 1984, when I was appointed general adviser for language development with Rotherham Local Education Authority, the first school on my list of visits was Broom Valley Infants. I was to examine and report on the teaching of reading.

There was a great feeling of anticipation that morning as I strolled up the drive of the infant school I had attended as a small child, in my dark inspectorial suit and black briefcase in hand. The school was no longer a vast and frightening place but just a small, square, featureless building, like so many post-war schools. I stood for a moment in the entrance hall staring down the corridor and thinking of my childhood, before informing the school secretary I had an appointment with the head-teacher. I took a deep breath. The smell of cabbage and floor polish had lingered – and so, I was soon to discover, had my teacher. Miss Greenhalgh was still there.

'I'm very pleased you have done so well, Gervase,' she told me. I ballooned with pride. 'Yes, you've done very well, very well indeed.' There was a short pause before Miss Greenhalgh added, 'Because you weren't on the top table, were you?'

She was right, I wasn't on the top table. But I did well in my examinations and went on to become an examiner myself. I was often amused by the unconscious humour of candidates. In response to one English Literature paper on the famous Shakespeare play, a candidate wrote: 'When Julius Caesar was on his way to the capital, he was set upon by a group of senators who were jealous of him and he was stabbed to death. His best friend was the last to stab the emperor and Caesar cried as he died: "Up yours, Brutus!".' One young hopeful, in response to a question about the character of Hamlet, wrote that 'he's a bit like the David Gower' and then wrote a masterful essay on the problems with the England cricket side.

chess

89

Epitaph

The school examiner, Mrs Best,
Who spent her life devising tests,
At last is sadly laid to rest,
And now in heaven *she's* assessed.

A question on a standardised reading test required children to place an appropriate word in the blank space: 'Pen is to ink as knife is to …' One child wrote 'back'.

—

Question How would you make soft water hard?
Answer Freeze it.

—

Asked in a test what steroids were used for, one secondary-aged pupil wrote, 'They're the metal things which hold the stair carpet in place.'

—

Question Complete the following expression: 'Where there's a will …'
Answer '… there's always a dead person.'

—

The numeracy test question in the national SAT tests asked the children to write answers in figures. Imagine my surprise when one of my pupils drew a string of matchstick men.

—

The SAT test paper in numeracy had a box, which said above: 'Show your working.'

One child had done an elaborate pencil sketch showing him busily working at his desk.

—

On a history test for children was the question : 'What do you know about Agricola?

One child answered, 'I know it is a fizzy drink for farmers.'

—

Answer on biology GCSE Paper: 'The appearance of the anus in evolution marked a massive breakthrough.'

—

On a Health and Safety Questionnaire:

Question 'What would you do if your little brother swallowed a key?'

Answer 'Get in through the window.'

—

The GCSE Chemistry paper asked: 'What advice would you give to someone handling dangerous chemicals?' The candidate's answer was nothing if succinct: 'Be careful.'

—

Question What is a myth?

Answer A female moth.

—

Question What proportion of the earth's surface is covered by sea?

Answer The blue bits.

—

Question What were the disadvantages of canal building?

Answer The bricks had to be built underwater.

—

The oil from the North Sea can also be used for frying chips.

—

During my lessons I get some of my work right and some of it wrong. Now I am getting most of my work right. Now my testes are much better.

—

'Can you name a bird with a long neck?' asked the teacher of her junior-aged class.

'Naomi Campbell,' came the prompt reply from the class wit.

—

Michelangelo spent most of his time on the ceiling.

—

Cleopatra's Needle was used to sew bodies into long white sheets and they became mummies.

—

I teach in a Yorkshire school and we were doing a project on the Tudors. I asked if anyone could recall the names of any of Henry VIII's wives.

'Well, there's Katherine of Harrogate and Ann of Leeds,' said one pupil.

—

Say briefly what you know about Lady Macbeth:

'She was a right old bitch.'

—

An inventive answer in an examination paper: 'When a bitch has puppies it's called alliteration.'

—

'What is the opposite of the word 'woe'?' asked the teacher

'Giddyup!' replied a pupil.

—

My young son, sitting the test to get into a prep school, was asked: 'What is the plural of deer?' He wrote 'darlings', His friend, asked to write the plural of 'spouse', wrote 'spice'. Both were successful, so I think the examiner recognised some imaginative potential.

—

'And with what do you connect Baden-Powell?' asked the teacher.

'A hyphen,' came the reply.

—

A simile is a colourful and interesting way of comparing things in poetry like 'she had a face like a sackful of dead ferrets.'

—

Eight-year-old: 'When the police catch a robber they put cuff links on him.'

—

A 'classic' is a really long and boring book that you have to read at school and sit an examination on.

—

Posthumous works of literature are those written after the author is dead.